Dutch Girl from Jakarta
From Indonesian Concentration Camp to Freedom

By Maria Zeeman

Copyright © 2019 by Maria Zeeman
All rights reserved

Cover Design, Frank Kearns, Carol Kearns

Cover Photo, Front, From Maria Zeeman

Cover Photo, Background, Jan-Pieter Nap. Used under the
   Creative Commons License:
   https://creativecommons.org/licenses/by-sa/1.0/deed.en

Photo of Maria Zeeman and her daughters from Southern California Public Radio (p. 113) © 2018 Southern California Public Radio. Used with permission.   All rights reserved.

First Edition
ISBN-13, 978-0-9984036-8-7

Published in the United States by Los Nietos Press
Downey, CA 90240

www.LosNietosPress.com
LosNietosPress@gmail.com

AUTHOR'S NOTE

This book was written to share, mostly with my family and friends, the incredible journey of my life over the last eighty-four years. Much of my story is mired in the aftermath of World War II and the Japanese concentration camp we resided in for almost four years. In American history, our suffering is often lost and most people do not even know about our journey through this tragedy of war. This piece of our past has been overshadowed by the Nazi concentration camps, and often times we are lost within the memories of such a terrible time in human history.

My hope in writing this memoir is for my family and friends to know what happened to us, and yet to also understand that regardless of the depth of tragedy one might face, we can still be incredibly loving, compassionate, and involved human beings. You will see the thread of love that entwines all the following stories.

We are not our experiences or our behaviors. We are who we are in our hearts. We are love, and that is the most important lesson I can share with you.

CONTENTS

Blessed with Grandbabies   1

MY LIFE

My Birth and Early Years   5
My Parents' Love Story   7
My Family   9
My Mother   12
My Father When I Was Young   14
My Uncle Pierre   17
The Beginning of World War II   19
Prisoner of War   23
Saving My Life   26
Favorite Toys   28
The End of the War   29
Uncle Pierre and the War   33
My First Stay in Holland   34
Memories of My Grandparents   37
My Monkey   39
Return to Holland 1949   42
Christmas in Holland   46
Working in Amsterdam   49
My Father's Retirement   52
Vacations as a Child   53
Meeting My Husband   55
Love in Beautiful Amsterdam   57
My Honeymoon   60
Married Life   61
Moving to Canada   62
My Guardian Angel   64
My Father's Death   66
My First Born   69
Motherhood and Marriage   71
The Breadwinner   74

Beatrix Is Born	76
Vacation in Canada	77
Traveling to California	79
The Scariest Time of My Life	81
Earthquake	82
Childhood Diseases	83
The Day We Got Hamsters	84
My Second Honeymoon	86
Emergency Surgery	88
Buying a House	90
The Poorest I've Ever Been	92
Choosing My Children's Names	94
My Last Job	96
Returning to Indonesia 1996	99
Never Too Old to Learn	108
Reflections on Indonesia	111
Sharing My Story on Stage	113

FAMILY

Having Many Siblings	119
In Honor of Our Parents	121
Our 1981 Reunion	122
My Brother Jan	124
My Brother Piet	127
My Sister Letty	128
Children and Grandchildren!	130
How I Almost Lost My Granddaughter	132
Las Vegas and Hawaii	134
Memory Lane and a River Trip	137
My Grandson's Wedding	140
My Favorite Birthday	141
A Wonderful Reunion	142
Our South American Relatives	144
Mother's Day 2018	146

MOMENTS
- What Makes Me Happy — 151
- My Special Talents — 152
- My Positive Influences as a Child — 153
- More Like Mother or Dad? — 155
- When I Am Hard on Myself — 156
- Concerts! — 157
- Resentments — 158
- Feeling Alone — 160
- I See You, But I Don't Know You — 161
- My Lively Child — 162
- Funny Family Folks — 164
- Rescued Again — 165
- Do I Believe in God? — 166
- Heroes — 168
- Advice on Raising Children — 169
- Competitions — 170
- Rain, Rain, Oh Rain! — 173
- Halloween Story — 174
- Mindless — 175
- A Mini Vacation to Los Angeles — 177
- My Bedroom — 179
- My Precious One — 180

EXTENDED "FAMILY"
- Like Mother, Like Daughter — 183
- How I Met My Honey — 185
- Lucas – Our Little "Houdini" — 188
- I Swear Lucas Has Nine Lives — 190
- My Honey was Lost! — 191
- My Honey — 192
- The End – But Not Yet — 194

Editor's Note — 197

Dutch Girl from Jakarta

BLESSED WITH GRANDBABIES

My full name is Maria Johanna Cornelia Zeeman and I'm eighty-four years old. Never in my younger life did I think that I would be an "old lady," and now I am. The amazing thing is that my family treated me with another grandson and two great-grandsons around my birthday.

Me with (l-r) great-grandsons Zane and William and grandson Reis 2019

My son Guillermo had another boy named Reis. He's healthy, lovely, and quite handsome already with his big blue eyes. He's a good baby, loved by everybody, especially by his sisters and brothers, his doting parents, their *Oma* (me) and their aunts Loretta and Beatrix.

The two great-grandbabies are from my daughter Loretta's sons. Garland's baby's name is Zane. Zane is the longest, least heavy baby of the three, also lovely. His dad is over six feet, so I'm sure he is going to be tall and handsome like his dad.

The other baby is from Casey, Loretta's oldest son. The baby's name is William, an old-fashioned English name. I love it. He was the biggest one when he was born, and still is. He has big blue eyes and a cute, sweet smile, with sturdy, strong little legs and lively body.

All three were born around my birthday in July 2019. Today, I have three children, ten grandchildren, and nine great-grandchildren.

The grandchildren call me and my children *Oma* and *Oma-ma*, which mean grandma and great-grandma in Dutch. Actually, "Oma-ma" is made up by Zane's sister Shayla (three years old). Great-grandmother was too long a name for her, she said. She is such a cute and determined girl that we use her version of the said name. She is also delighted with her new brother, and of course so are her parents.

Consider, it took me almost ten years after marriage to finally get my first baby! No wonder I feel so lucky, blessed, and rewarded today.

MY LIFE

MY BIRTH AND EARLY YEARS

My full name is Maria Johanna Cornelia Zeeman. I was born July 22, 1935, in a hospital in Padang on the island of Sumatra, Indonesia, the sixth of eight children. I was six pounds and healthy. There were no problems with my birth, my mother told me.

My father had hoped for another boy. There were already three living, beautiful daughters and two sons. However, my parents were happy that I was healthy, had blue eyes, and was another blonde.

My parents were citizens of the Netherlands, known as Holland. My oldest sister, Francisca (Fransje), was born in Holland after World War I. My second oldest sister, Petronella (Nellie), was born in Belgium.

My parents and two siblings moved to Indonesia when my father took a position as a Dutch harbor pilot. Indonesia used to be the Dutch East Indies for three hundred years and was ruled by the Dutch. My father's job required two-year rotations with other harbor pilots on other islands. That is why we six younger children were born in different cities in Indonesia.

Petrus (Piet), Claar Maria, and Johannes (Jan) were born before me. Violeta (Letty) was born at home, two years after me, also in Padang. And Beatrix (Trixie) was born four years after me in Batavia, on the island of Java, presently known as Jakarta, Indonesia.

Jan was thirteen months older than me and was quite sickly for a while. So, I was mostly with my oldest sister or our *baboe* (nanny). I was a good baby they said. Even my father was happy with me. We were always close. I adored him.

I don't remember much from my very young life. I was a very happy child my mother always said. It was soon after my sister Letty was born that we moved to Batavia. We lived right near the ocean and very close to the harbor. There were several big houses for the officers who worked there and several houses for the captains and other employees of the Dutch ships that stopped there, so they could use them when they came on land.

I remember when I was four or five years old that we lived in such a big house with four big bedrooms, one big living room and a big dining room. We also had a big porch. My father would leave early in the morning to work and my mother was always home. Jakarta, Indonesia, has tropical weather, very hot. We had a native woman who woke us and got us dressed. Then we saw Mam (our mother) and had breakfast all together.

My brother Jan and I would always play together on the floor of the front porch. It was a marble floor and cool to play on. We played with marbles and cards. We usually didn't play wild games because it was too hot. Mam was often with us, but she was usually busy with my two younger sisters. I also remember that she sang songs. I loved that. I remember that we were happy then.

We always played together because there were very few children close by. Most of my older siblings went to school. A bus picked them up at six in the morning and brought them home by one thirty. At two o'clock we had to be quiet for two hours and play or rest in the house. That's the hottest time of the day. I remember that I usually played mostly with my brother Jan. He went to first grade.

My father worked on the ships, bringing them in to port from the ocean. He had a loud voice, but he was very kind. He would tell us stories, so many! We loved it. Mother read us stories from the books, also many. We loved those too. She could sing so nice. Often religious songs. They all say that I was very happy as a small child, that I played so well with my brother Jan and later with my two younger sisters.

MY PARENTS' LOVE STORY

The year was 1920. My mother and her best girlfriends were eighteen years old, having fun, walking and flirting with the sailors on the quay in Amsterdam. All three girls worked for the telephone company and felt pretty special. They were high school graduates, which was unusual. At that time, high school was mainly for boys. The girls had a job that was both good and fun.

My mother told us that she saw this handsome, sturdy, and buff sailor with deep brown eyes and a lusty laugh. He came closer. They talked, looked in each other eyes and were in a world of their own. The girls laughed and teased them. "Don't be too serious, Maria. He's just a sailor."

My mother came from a well-to-do family. They lived in the city. Her father was a diamond cutter, part time. Her parents also had a cigar store which was run by my grandmother. My mother was one of the few girls who went to school to get an equivalent of a high school diploma. My mother had an older brother, Pierre.

My paternal grandfather was a traveling salesman. His wife was a fisherman's daughter with little education. They lived in Hilversum, Holland, and had two sons—my dad and his brother Johannes. Later, my grandfather divorced his wife and married a woman from Germany.

My dad, who was a year older than my mother, was sent to work on the ships as a deck boy at age thirteen, so he was tough. His brother stayed with their mother. My dad was strong and loyal to his work but he had dreams of becoming an engineer or captain on a ship. Then terror struck Holland. The first world war began. The ship he was on hit an explosive bomb and only five men survived. Thank God he was one of them. As restitution he got an invitation from the Dutch government to study sailing and navigation. He became a first mate and rose to captain.

My mother was still innocent when she met my father, but they got married within a year in July 1920. They loved each other and wanted many children.

My parents always showed us how important it is to love, trust, and respect each other through thick and thin. Each Mother's Day my father gave my mother a BIG bouquet of flowers and said, "Thank you for giving me so many children. I love you." It sure helped us get through some very difficult times. I consider myself lucky that I was granted the parents I had.

(Clockwise from upper left) Petrus, Letty, Mother, Piet, Nellie, Jan, Me, Claar, Francisca. Trixie was not yet born.

MY FAMILY

My father and mother were married in 1920. There was a depression, and my mother didn't want him to go on the ocean again but to get a job on shore. This was impossible. He tried many jobs but nothing was adequate to support him, his wife, and now a daughter. They moved to Belgium. But there too was a recession after the war. It was a struggle.

He migrated to the USA while my mother and sister remained behind. He worked in the woods somewhere in California, getting the big trunks of the trees down the river. But he had to wait a full year before he could bring his family over. That was too hard for him.

He was so lonesome there. Even though he spoke English and French, as well as Dutch, there wasn't much companionship on the job. There were no women or children, only men. So, before the year was over, he returned to Belgium. He stood in front of my mother's apartment in Antwerp, Belgium, and surprised her.

In 1924 he was offered a job as a harbor pilot, and he could take his family with him. So, they boarded a big ship and made the six-week trip to Jakarta, Indonesia. At first it was good for my dad, but my mother couldn't get used to the change. The food is totally different. The main dish is rice prepared in many ways, no potatoes or carrots. Also, no apples or pears or cherries. Lots of different fruit, like *rambutan*, *duku*, mangos, many kinds of *pisang* (bananas), coconuts, *mangistan*, papaya, *djeruk*, and many more.

We, the children, didn't want to eat what my mother wanted. We liked the food in Indonesia and loved all the fruit. There were many different animals and insects too, including the *tjitjaks*, who ran on the walls at night to catch the mosquitoes and other bugs while chirping "*tokey*" quite loud. Those BIG red ants, we played with. There were no dogs to guard the house, but geese. There were no cats, but little monkeys, and many more.

Mother had a hard time at first. Except for my two oldest sisters, the other six of us were born in Indonesia. We moved every two years because my father's job required a rotation with the other harbor pilots. We were very happy, loved the food and fruits, didn't know any other way, loved our way of living. And of course, eventually my mother got used to it and loved it too. So, we were always together, didn't have many friends or particular schools we bonded with because we were always moving. We depended on each other for about everything.

(l-r) Francisca, Nellie, Piet, Claar, Jan, Me, Letty, Trixie

MY MOTHER

Maria Johanna Cornelia Francois

My mother, Maria Johanna Cornelia Francois, was born in Amsterdam, Netherlands, on July 28, 1901, and left us in 1995. Her parents were fairly well-to-do and were very proud of her. They sent her to what was the equivalent of high school, which was not done often for girls at that time in Holland. She worked for the telephone company until she got married.

My parents wanted many children. Well, they got eight children. I was the sixth one. They were happily married. I remember my mother mostly as a very kind and sweet lady, intelligent and strong. She always knew how to say the right thing at the right time.

Later Mam was my friend as well as my sweet mother. We already played bridge when I was very young and kept it up through many years. When my dad was working, we often went to the movies as well. We were very close in spite of the many years when I lived elsewhere and later emigrated. We saw each other at least once a year and kept in touch by letter and tape.

I loved her so much and still often think of her. Mam lived the last years of her life in Lachine, Canada, with my youngest sister. The last two months she was in a hospital but was still fully alert. I played bridge with her two weeks before she died. I went home to California. Then my sister called me and said, "Come back if you can."

I came right away, and when I came to her, she said, "Oh, you came," and smiled. She lost consciousness and passed away peacefully, holding my oldest sister's hand and mine, with six of her children around. She finally went to her husband.

My mother Maria in the back seat

Petrus Wilmus Zeeman

MY FATHER WHEN I WAS YOUNG

My father, Petrus Wilmus Zeeman, was born in January 1900 and passed away in 1962. When I was a child, I remember that Pa was an important person. He always had a uniform on, white with stars and lines on it. He looked so handsome and strong. He worked on the ships to navigate them through the harbor. He was an honorable man with many patriotic feelings.

We lived then in the Dutch East Indies, which is now Indonesia. I remember that Pa always told stories about animals, other countries, or different people, and many others. He was a great storyteller. Everybody liked to listen to him. He looked rough and had a strong voice, but he was gentle and kind. Pa never hit us. All he had to do look mad and we were sorry for whatever he was mad about.

He had rules! Up at five in the morning, eat breakfast all together, free time for lunch, eat dinner together at a big dining room table. My parents sat at the head of the table and didn't eat with us. We each had a turn to tell what happened that day, or tell what was on our mind, starting with the oldest and finishing with the youngest. Then they would sit at a smaller table together. We could play then for forty-five minutes, take a shower and get ready for bed. The four youngest went to bed at seven o'clock. The four oldest went to bed at eight.

One day all that changed. Everybody was nervous and my dad came home to tell us that we had to get ready to go in the car. He drove to the big city and there the Japanese soldiers took him away. He said, "We are at war. Be good, careful, and stick together and be good for your mother."

I was almost six years old. I saw him again three and a half years later—after the war ended. I didn't recognize him at first. He looked so small, his face was ugly with brown welts and he had a long gray beard. But when he called me and looked me in the eye, I knew who he was. He had tears in his eyes. I felt very strange and uncertain. He looked so different and was different. Later I found out that he was a courageous, strong, and very righteous man—helping the other men and boys in the camp.

He always showed his love to my mother. Every Mother's Day he would come with a big bunch of flowers and thank her for giving him so many children. I respected and adored him always.

At sixty-two years old he died. I will miss him forever.

My father in Indonesia with his colleagues

MY UNCLE PIERRE

I have two uncles. My father's younger brother, Johannes, we called *Oom* Jo in Dutch. He lived in Holland.

My mother's older brother, our *Oom* Pierre, was also born in Holland but later lived in Hong Kong and Indonesia. *Oom* Pierre was not only smart, stern, honest, proud, and well educated, he was handsome and tall, spoke several languages.

Oom Pierre and Tante Violet with my cousins Pieter and Walter

After WW I there were few good jobs in Holland. While my father took a job as a harbor pilot in Indonesia, *Om* Pierre moved to Hong Kong and worked for the Hollandse Handelbank (Dutch International Bank).

He was the BIG boss. They all liked him and, of course, he spoke Chinese as well as English, and more. He worked there a few years when he met Violet. She was an Indian lady from India and dark-skinned. At that time no white men were allowed to marry anyone who wasn't white.

Oom Pierre did marry her. They demoted him and he was sent to Batavia (presently Jakarta). He got a job at a regular Dutch bank. It was a demotion but he wanted Violet more than the good job and the higher salary. That's when we saw them and got to know them better. Our aunt, *Tante* Vi, was a lovely lady, very sweet, smart, and funny. *Oom* Pierre was quiet, serious, and stern.

They had two sons, my cousins Pieter and Walter. They always had to study, do extra work. *Oom* Pierre had HIGH hopes for them. The boys were allowed to play with us at our house or in the park, but they only asked my sister Letty to come over to their house, sometimes to stay overnight.

Letty had polio as a small kid, walked with an iron brace and funny shoes. She also limped. *Tante* Vi was always so kind to her. If you have five sisters and two brothers, it's very nice to have someone pay extra attention to just you. *Oom* Pierre read books with Letty. Their own sons were sometimes jealous and play-teased Letty by walking behind her with a limp, giggling. *Oom* Pierre always came to her rescue.

THE BEGINNING OF WORLD WAR II

I felt so big and looked anxious going to first grade. We lived too far from the school. There was no kindergarten at that time. My brother Jan already did go to school on the bus. We lived close to the ocean in a big white house. Connected to the house were many small rooms in a row. We had five servants who were with us for many years. Each had their own room. Then there was a room for the kitchen, washing and ironing, bathroom, toilet room, a room for the bikes and toys, and a room for the "cleaning up" equipment. I shared a room with Letty, my younger sister, in the house. We liked to be together.

Me (l) and brother Jan in Indonesia

All the floors were of marble, that made it cool. The temperature in Indonesia is very high, especially at midday. We often played at home on the cool floor, wearing light summer clothes and in bare feet, with cards or dice, monopoly, jacks, and other games. We played mostly together, because there were no other children close by. Letty, Trix, Jan, and I were the four youngest in the family. We played together and were competitive!

My older siblings usually did other things. Sometimes they played with us too. That was really fun. We also went to the waterfront and played there, always staying together. At night, promptly at six o'clock, my parents sat at the dinner table, one at each end. We children sat four on each side of the table. The food was cooked and served by the *baboe* (servant). My mother told her what to cook.

While we were having dinner, we all got a turn to tell what was on our mind, about school, or things that happened. When we were finished the *baboe* set a small table for Mam and Pa and served them, so they could talk together privately. Then we all did what we wanted until bedtime. That was a fun and happy time.

One day, even at six years old, I felt that something was wrong. Everybody was so serious, talking softly. They didn't want to upset us, we four smaller kids. Soon the terrible change came. We never could have guessed that this was the end of our happy and peaceful family time together.

One early morning in May my dad came home, nervous and upset, told all of us to get ready to go to the city. I was always very close to my parents. I told them many things and always got answers. But the day we left our home suddenly, in 1941, all changed. I didn't understand why my parents were so scared and rushing us to the car. Why didn't they tell us that something was wrong?

We had a Ford car. Today I wonder how we all could sit in that car. We were a family of ten and one of the servants came with us. That made eleven people. We were sitting on top of each other. And—we took our pregnant cat along!

We were packed in and scared. It was eerily quiet on the road. My father drove, everybody was very still. We didn't know what was happening. My parents and two older sisters were so subdued. Very strange. Then our cat started to meow very loudly in a scary way. My father had to stop on the side of the road. There were no other cars or any living souls around. Our poor cat was having her babies. We had to leave her. We all cried, including my very rough and strong dad, but he said we had to go and to pray that somebody would find her and take care of her.

I remember that we could hardly breathe—we sat on top of each other. But at long last we arrived at a big house somewhere in the city, Batavia (Jakarta). There were Japanese soldiers who let us in the house and assigned us our rooms. Our *baboe* could stay and she helped us. We were very close to her, especially my two younger sisters and my brother Jan.

A Japanese officer came and yelled at my dad the next day, ordered him outside to go in a bus. We saw other men in the bus. What were they doing and why did he have to go with them? It was all very scary, but they let our *baboe* stay to make food for us.

This went on for some time. Nobody knew where Pa was. The solders came in the house, sometimes even ate with us at the table. That was very strange. They ate with their hands instead of with a fork and spoon, but they seemed to like our food. They burped and slurped which was also very strange for us. They even washed themselves differently and they hardly ever smiled or seemed to be happy.

One time the soldier who ate at the table began to sing in a very eerie voice. I remember it well, it was very strange, I had never heard anything like it. I'm sure none of my family did either. After that he never returned. We did not see him again.

My mother and three older sisters were constantly together. Nobody did anything in particular. We just sat and roamed around the house. We four little ones did nothing. Nobody seemed to care or know what to do or what to expect.

Then Jan, my brother, went to the *campong*--where the Indonesians live in small villages. They were also under the authority of the Japanese soldiers. We spoke the natives' language and they were very protective of us. Of course, Jan was not allowed to go to the native village, or anywhere else other than the house.

The day that Jan and I snuck out, something bad happened in the village. We heard screaming and loud crying. A bunch of the young men were called together. We were hiding and very scared. Then we saw one of the soldiers get one of the men and with his big sword cut his hand off.

The people who were hiding us kept us very quiet and took us home as soon as they could. That same night a few solders were running through our rooms. All nine of us were in my mother's bed shivering.

The soldiers stomped through our house. We still never said a word about what we saw that afternoon. It was so scary and the next morning my mother insisted that they take us to the camp. Our life changed again. It wasn't as scary but it wasn't good. We never could have guessed how awful it was going to be.

When my brother Piet turned twelve, the soldiers took him away to the men's camp. Then we were eight.

The first Christmas we had in the camp without our father and Piet was rough, but my loving mother somehow collected some silver paper. She told us to make a present from it. She made us draw a name so everybody had to make something pretty—a necklace, a doll, a dress, or flower. We did and we had a good time, sang sweet songs, and prayed for our dad and brother.

We had love and joy and Mam said, "That is what Christmas is about."

PRISONER OF WAR

Tjideng Camp 1942 – 1946

After we left that big house in Jakarta, we moved to Tjideng camp. We were put in a small house; here we could still cook and we had a bathroom for the first eight months. Once a week we were allowed to go out of the camp and buy food or other things with money, or clothes or jewelry. Our problem was that we had no money or anything to sell or trade.

My oldest sister Fransje was pretty smart and asked my mother what she missed the most during the first world war. My mother said, "Soap."

Fransje had already worked for a little while before the war and knew other people. One of them was Ma San Jaw, a Chinese man who was free outside. Fransje asked him to get her soap, and she started to sell the soap inside the camp. We all helped, and soon we could pay Ma San Jaw some money. He got us more soap to sell, and so we were able to get some food.

Then all of a sudden, the soldiers closed the gates and put a double fence around the camp. A soldier would walk around it so nobody could get out. Fransje could never thank Ma San Jaw for helping us, so she threw a thank you note over the gates. She and four other women were caught trying to communicate with outsiders.

Fransje and the other women later came back, and we saw what they had done to Fransje. She was blue all over. Apparently, they knew how to hit so that it hurt a lot, but there was no blood. Her legs, arms, and back were black and blue and painful for a very long time. Fransje told us nothing about what happened except for this very tall blond lady who was put in a doghouse. Nobody knows whatever happened to her.

One morning we all had to come forward and give the soldiers all that we had in valuables. They were very rough in taking off the rings and other jewelry. Some of the women hid their valuables, but the soldiers seemed to know where to look. It was awful and very degrading.

Then they rounded up all of the dogs that anyone kept as pets. The animals were all thrown into a big truck, and we cried silently as we watched them slaughter our animals. They made us keep our eyes open.

We were now not allowed to cook or have running water. Every day we went to the big building and received a handful of food. In the morning we got a slice of bread which was like leather; but we could chew on it for a long time.

Early every morning, and again in the afternoon, we had to stand in rows of ten people deep to bow to the captain. There was about a foot between each row. Soldiers would walk down each row, and if someone wasn't standing straight, that person got hit.

We were made to listen to the captain who stood high on a pedestal. Then we would stand straight, bow down deep and stand up again. In the beginning it wasn't so bad, but when Captain Kenichi Sonei took over, it was often very bad. When he gave the order to bow, he would make us stay bent over for a long time. If anyone fell, they beat them.

All eight of us children were with my mother until my brother Piet reached the age of twelve. Then they took him away. We never saw him again until after the war. Other families were put into our house with us. We had a bed and two big wooden cases for our family to lay or sit on.

Mam, Fransje, Nel, and Claar slept on the bed. Jan, Letty, Trix, and I slept on those cases. Fransje stayed home with my mother and the four younger members of our family.

Nel was seventeen years old and her job was to work with the *shouw ploeg* carrying heavy things and cleaning the small ditches that ran in front of the houses. Everybody had to use these ditches as a latrine and a place to throw up. It always smelled so bad, and it was a hard job to keep clean. They used the young girls for that.

Claar was with the eleven-year-olds. She had to clean the big black drums they cooked the food in. She would climb into the drums to scrub the bottom. As long as she had shoes, she would bring scraps of food to us in her shoes. Later, when there were no shoes, she put the food under her toes.

We four little ones did nothing. We had no school, no church, no medical help. Slowly we ran out of clothes and shoes—but we always had soap.

Sometimes I think that being part of a large family helped to keep us safe. My mother and I got real sick with tropical sores during the last months, but my sisters always made sure that we showed up to bow down to Captain Sonei.

SAVING MY LIFE

In my early years, especially during the nearly four years in the camp, the most important people in my life were my mother and my oldest sister Fransje. Without them I wouldn't be here.

The third year of the camp, I got extremely sick. We were not supposed to get sick! It started with a terrible earache. We had no doctors and there wasn't any medicine either. So, they cleaned it by rolling up strips of sheets and shoving them into my ear to pull the infection and puss out. It hurt so much that I often pretended that I couldn't get up so that I didn't have to go. But Mam or Fransje got me up. I had to, or the soldiers would have sent me away, and we knew that we never saw those people again who were sent away. So, they knew I had to get up and pretend I was fine. I had to walk properly while on my way, and on the way back after those "treatments." It was the worst pain I had ever felt, well, until my leg got sick.

Soon after, I got a sore on my leg. It got worse and worse, and it was so painful and stank to high heaven. Once again, they took me to those women. More and more people got those tropical abscesses. They were so painful and all anyone could do was try to keep it clean any way they could in that awful place. Oh, my goodness, I wished I could just lay there and never get up, but they made me, Mam and Fransje. I didn't want to and was so sad and felt so hopeless, but they got me up, day after day. I was in such agony, but I did it for them. That was the worst pain I ever felt—until the next thing.

It seems strange for me now, as I remember it, because I always played bridge with my mother and two oldest sisters. One plays with a partner, so you always need four players. Claar didn't like to play much. I always loved it, even when I had the painful sore on my leg and agonizing ear aches. Bridge helped me to not think about my pain. And bridge is a difficult game. One has to remember the fifty-two cards and understand the other players.

We four young ones also played the game, but then it was a lot of pretend. I realized later that it's a difficult game, so I wasn't dumb ever, just uneducated because of my years in the prison camp. I always thought later that bridge and my mother's soft singing saved our lives.

I often wondered how Mam and Fransje could have done what they did. They saw my agony and pain, why not let it go? Many others died or lost their limbs. But my mother and Fransje never gave up. They saved my life. I didn't know it then, but I sure know it now.

FAVORITE TOYS

When I was five years old, I got a doll. I was so happy! She was soft, had a very pretty face. She wore a beautiful dress, blue with polka dots on it. I loved that doll, called her "my Princess." I had Princess for many years. Mam and Fransje made new clothes for her so she could also look like a school girl, or wear sport pants and jacket, all in red.

I took her with me to the camp. I was lucky to have her. She comforted me many times when we were prisoners of war.

Later in the prison camp, Fransje cut a doll out of a magazine and strengthened it by pasting it on cardboard and cutting it out. Then she took a strip of cardboard and pasted it on the back of the doll so she could stand up. Then she made paper dresses and more for me.

That was very nice for me. The last year of our confinement I could hardly walk and just laid around often waiting for my angel to come for me and take me away. Yes, my two dolls were a real treasure. I was also lucky to have sisters, a brother, and a mother to try to make me feel better. They were always kind to me.

THE END OF THE WAR

One day we heard the soldiers leave and we knew the war was over. I was nine years old by then and my mother and I were very sick. We had been living in this Japanese concentration camp in Indonesia for three and a half years. I had not seen my father and older brother Piet for all that time.

My family went back to our spot in the camp and waited. Somehow, Fransje got hold of a banana and I will never forget how she fed it to our mother with a tiny spoon. We were all hungry, but Fransje gave the whole banana to our mother to save her life.

And it did.

Later, we saw packages being thrown from the American planes. The parcels falling from the sky were filled with food, cans, candies, lipstick, and cigarettes. These last two things I had never even seen before. We tried to eat the lipstick.

"We will eat again," said my mother, "and someday you will go to school." I was amazed and awestruck. I still didn't know what a school was, or what a doctor or hospital was either. Then we saw a doctor who gave my mother and me some medicine. Her sore was not as big as mine and it got better soon. Mine did not.

Ma Son Jaw finally found us and took my mother, Jan, Letty, and Trix on a train to Bandung. He knew that my father and brother were there. Fransje, Nel, and Claar had to stay with me until I got better. This took two more months. Then our Chinese friend took us to Bandung to join the rest of the family.

I had not seen my father or brother Piet in four years. I did not even recognize them. They were emaciated and broken-looking. Pa had awful scars on every inch of his body, even the soles of his feet. He had a huge swollen nose and a long, scraggly grey beard. I did not recognize him at first. We all reunited again at last.

Many years later I learned that when my brother was being punished for eating a dog (because they were so hungry), my father asked the Japanese soldiers to punish him instead. Pa was put on a pole, in the hot sun, and beaten severely. That he why he looked so terrible.

My dad and Piet were in Bandung in an all-men camp. My family was allowed to live in a big house right next to the camp. Many of the men stayed in the camp, as people did in the camp we just left, because there was nowhere to go.

The young Indonesians were now against us. Captain Sonei and all the Japanese soldiers were from the beginning telling them to hate the Dutch people and to fight for independence, create a Republic of Indonesia. Those young Indonesian men formed groups and killed many white people. It was so dangerous. Some of the men who wandered out of the camp were shot by those groups.

In the camp, nobody had money or anything of value. There were also many young boys with no one to take care of them. On the other side of our house were Gurkha soldiers from India to protect us.

Somehow Pa arranged for a military plane to fly seven of us to Batavia—my parents, Claar, Jan, Lettie, Trixie, and me. My father had already sent Piet back to Holland right away for his education. Nel and Fransje stayed behind. Nel helped with the sick soldiers, as a nursing aid. Fransje married Jan, a young man who had been in the same camp as my father, and they had a child. Later they all returned to Holland.

Our flight was so dangerous. We sat on the floor with a thick rope that was tied in the front and back of the plane to hold on. The plane flew so low, we could see the tops of the trees and sometimes we thought we would hit the mountain tops.

We made it and were put up in a house in the city. My father had to report immediately to the harbor. They had no one to bring the ships in safely.

This was the first time we youngest ones went to school. My brother Jan went to second grade, but my two younger sisters and I had never yet been to school. So, we went to grade one. We were so happy to go and finally we learned more things. My sister Fransje had taught us some words, letters, and other things in the beginning of the camp.

But again, it was rather dangerous, too, where we were now. We walked hand in hand for one block, crossed the bridge and walked another block and a half to the school. There were very few white people. The native Indonesians were our friends we thought, and many were, but not that group of young men. We didn't understand that the big kids hated us.

One day we were on the bridge and saw a plank going down the river. On the plank was a dead white lady with her breasts cut off and nailed to the plank. It was so awful. We told our father. Then he said that he would send us to Holland on the first ship out. We were to stay home until then.

A few days later he was driven to the harbor with a few other officers as usual, but that evening he didn't come home. Oh, we were so scared. My mother sat with us holding hands and asking God to take care of our dad. Then at four o'clock in the morning he came home all dirty and bloody. His small bus was attacked and they stole anything they could get their hands on. Pa said that he slapped the hand that wanted to take his wallet. He recognized the man as one of the guards from the harbor. They took off. The car was disabled and the four men walked home. It was a long walk. One of them had a broken ankle, the others were all hurt, but they all made it home.

Shortly after this my father was able to arrange for the first ship available to take my mother and us five youngest children to Holland—Claar, Jan, Letty, Trixie, and me. My two older sisters stayed in Jakarta and my father had already sent my older brother Piet to Holland.

We traveled on a military ship used to transport servicemen, the *Boschfontein*. We slept in the hull of the ship in canvas hammocks strung five high. Each had a small blanket. Row after row of beds. It was rough weather almost from the beginning and then there was a terrible storm.

At one point the ship lost its power and we drifted around in the storm. Everybody had to stay below in bed. We all got sick, and they closed all the doors. We couldn't go on deck. It was horrible. We all threw up hanging off our beds. I was in the fourth bed up. The stink was horrendous. We were rolling and bumping on the beds. The few who got off their beds fell down. The storm lasted almost two full days. When the ocean calmed down, we still could not go on deck.

At long last we went through the Suez Canal and got off the boat to get some clothes. Warm underwear, a dress, shoes and socks, a coat, toothbrush, comb, washcloth and a small towel, and some pretty pins for our hair. There was a water pump outside for us to clean ourselves, and they gave us soap too. Then we put the clothes on. That felt so good, even though it was very hot. We were told we would need the coat later. All we had was one panty. I remember that the coat I got was purple. I thought it was the most beautiful coat I ever saw. We liked everything. All together it took close to six weeks at sea before we arrived in Amsterdam.

UNCLE PIERRE AND THE WAR

When the war broke out in 1942, the Japanese's soldiers took *Oom* Pierre to a concentration camp, but left *Tante* Vi and the boys out for about a year. Later they took our older cousin Piet and put him in a boy's camp. About a year later *Tante* Vi was also put in a camp with her younger son Walter.

They all survived and went to Holland. In Holland at that time there was no prejudice against dark-skinned people, only uneducated people.

Oom Pierre died after a few years. *Tante* Vi lived for another seven years in a home for seniors. She was happy. Pieter became a psychiatrist in Holland and Walter an engineer who liked to travel. Walter ended up here in California with his lovely wife Hedy. We do keep in contact. They are the only relatives of my age left in California.

MY FIRST STAY IN HOLLAND

My father had to remain in Indonesia because there were hardly any pilots left to bring the ships into the harbors. Indonesia consists of over a thousand islands, the currents are strong, different. He taught some of the Indonesians to do the job. He stayed because he had a few more years before his pension came in. Five of us children went to Holland with our mother on the first ship available in 1946.

Holland was a disappointment. Nobody was expecting us. They really didn't know what to do with us. There were many orphans on the ship. After a full day of confusion, they took us in busses somewhere. On the bus we saw people with strange hats—some with feathers, some flat ones, and some berets. We never had seen those things before and we thought they were the funniest sights ever.

We also saw women with no hair, some totally bald. When we left our camp in Indonesia, there were also women with no hair. They were the women who worked for us and settled many things with the Japanese Commander. So, we were always very kind to them and greeted them with kindness and love. But in Holland we were told not to do that because the women there were shaven because they had gone out with the Germen soldiers.

We lived in Holland for about nine months. It was very difficult for us. We five children had never been in Holland and all of the people were strangers to us. Even our grandparents. Our two older sisters had remained in Indonesia. Francisca stayed in Indonesia because she had met and married her husband Jan there. Nel was working as a nurse's aide with all of the injured soldiers. My brother Piet was somehow placed in a college by our father. He wanted Piet to become a sea captain, as he was.

There was no place where we five children and our mother could all live together. Mam and Claar could stay with a cousin in a one-bedroom apartment. Trixie, my youngest sister, went to a family with twelve children in Diemen. Jan, my brother, went to Grandpa Zeeman, my father's father. I went to live with a couple in Bussum, (total strangers to me), who had opted to take care of a child from Indonesia. My sister Letty went to live with our uncle and aunt, *Oom* Jo and *Tante* Miep.

We had never been away from our mother before, so that was very hard. We were spread out, all over Holland. We missed each other very much, especially our mother. And Mam too was very unhappy without us and her two older daughters who were still in Indonesia.

We all went to school. I think that Trix, my youngest sister, was the luckiest one. All of the twelve children in the family where she lived were nice to her, and also their parents. Jan was OK, I think, and Claar also. Letty had *Tante* Miep and *Oom* Jo.

It was a nightmare for me. My mother never told us about men and/or sex. I was only nine years old and I came in this strange family. There were no other children. I had to go back to grade one and I was very weak. They made me go to the early mass before going to class. I often fainted and had to go to the last row in the church to lie down.

The teachers and most of the kids were nice. In one month, I went to second grade. But at home it was terrible. I had to eat what they made. They didn't want to know that I wasn't used to any of the food they gave me. In Indonesia, one eats rice and very well-cooked meat and very different vegetables, fruit, juices and more. I often had stomach aches and threw up.

I never slept with adults in the same bed before. In the camp the we four youngest children slept on two big wooden cases. My mother and my three oldest sisters slept in the only bed we had. Right after the war we slept wherever we could. We moved around constantly until we went on the ship to Holland. On this military ship we slept in hammocks stacked five high.

Now I was in a regular bed. I had no idea that they slept like that. I could feel her breasts and often him too. I was very uncomfortable. In the evening Uncle Ben (that's what I had to call him) went for a walk for about half an hour and I had to go with him. I was weak and could hardly keep up with him.

He would hold me so close; later he said I had to put my hand in his pocket to keep me steady. There was a hole in it so you know what I had to feel. Oh, my God, I was so uncomfortable, I didn't dare to say anything. Then they wanted to keep me. Oh no, Mother, please no.

I prayed and prayed to God to help me. And—He did. I got the chicken pox (again). I had had it in the camp terribly bad. I got it all over again. It was also in my hair, etc.

They called my mother to pick me up. They couldn't handle a sick child! I was so happy. I ended up also in Amsterdam. The fourth month we were in Holland they had an apartment for us in Amsterdam. I remember that I thanked God. I was so happy. I never told anybody about this. Much later I realized that they had been molesting me.

My mother never thought about those things. She was often so sad by what her children went through. I couldn't talk about those things with her. Then one day people found a small apartment for us in Amsterdam. Mam and we five kids were together in a one-bedroom apartment. For the next six months we lived there and we went to school. I did the first, second, and third grade in that time.

In Amsterdam they put me in third grade. I had to forgo all the fun classes, like physical education, singing, drawing and others. All I had was grammar, reading, math, and history. I had very little contact with the other children. When I went home, I had to take the tram, because I couldn't walk that far home yet. Nobody gets up for a child. Even when I fainted, I had to sit on the steps near the tram engineer. My mother picked me up often from the tram stop, or some of my other siblings did. No, it wasn't a good time at all.

MEMORIES OF MY GRANDPARENTS

The first time I saw my grandparents I was almost ten years old. They lived in Holland. I did hear about them from my parents, but we lived in the Dutch East Indies, now Indonesia.

My mother had nice parents. She talked about them often. *Opa*, my grandpa, was a diamond cutter; his wife ran a cigarette and cigar store. Grandpa was also often drunk, but he was a "happy" drunk. My mother told us that *Oma* would pick up his paychecks to prevent him from spending it all at his favorite bar. In spite of that, they were happy together. They had a son and a daughter and they always wanted the best for them.

My two oldest sisters saw our grandparents once when they went on vacation to Holland before the war. They had many funny and happy stories about them. They loved them, were very kind and good to them.

Three generations—sister Letty, Oma, and Mam in Amsterdam

When I came to Holland after the World War II, I met *Oma*, my maternal grandmother, for the first time. She was very sweet, but also very old. My grandpa, her husband, died just by the end of the war and we never had the fortune of meeting him. We were in Holland for eight months and then returned to Indonesia.

I also met my father's father in Holland. He was also old. He looked a little like my dad, but he didn't know me and tried to be friendly. I wasn't used to any men and felt strange and a bit scared. He had only one eye. He lost it when lightning struck him while he was in his back yard.

My father's mother was not there anymore. Grandpa Zeeman had remarried and had a daughter who was as old as my oldest sister Francisca. It was very uncomfortable, and for some reason nobody liked her. She was my father's half-sister, my aunt, I understood. She had a lot of clothes and toys. We had only the bare minimum after Indonesia. We didn't understand why she had so much and didn't let us play or touch any of these wonderful things. We were a big family and we shared everything. My dad wasn't with us, so, he couldn't explain, and my mother didn't want to say anything

I got to know my mother's mother well when we returned for good to Holland in 1949. *Oma* was a real sweetheart like my mother. She could play chess and checkers and tried to teach us. I loved her and was often with her.

I was married and living in Almelo when Mam went to visit my siblings who had moved to Canada. My father stayed in Amsterdam. *Oma* got sick and was moved into a home for older people. I came to visit her every Friday and stayed over the weekend. She thought I was her daughter and I let her believe that. We talked about the "old times" and she was so happy. When my father came to visit her, she would ask me, "Who is that man? He comes often, is nice, and takes me outside." My father came often to take her outside.

My mother came back from Canada as soon as she could when she heard that her mother was dying. She never made it. *Oma* went peacefully holding my hand. The last words were, *"Dag lieve Mies, je vader wacht op mij."* (Bye darling Mies, your dad is waiting for me). Mies was my nickname. At least I was there when she passed away.

For some reason, we saw little of my father's family and never got to really know them. I was busy with study and work. Later I was a bit sorry that I didn't make more of an effort.

MY MONKEY

I was glad that Pa sent for us to return to Indonesia in 1947. This time we went to Surabaya and stayed there until August-1949. That is still on the island of Java, much farther away from Batavia (Jakarta). We went to school on a bus because we lived again near the harbor near my father's work. The bus picked us up at six o'clock in the morning and brought us back by one thirty in the afternoon.

We had lunch together, after that we had two hours of rest or play quietly. It was a good time. We went to the Catholic schools. The nuns were very nice and much more understanding, of course. The kids also. Most went through what we went through.

Around my eleventh birthday I got my period. I was so scared, and thought I had done something really bad. I couldn't talk to my mother. My oldest sister Fransje came to live with us and she understood what was wrong with me. She told me that Claar, who was five years older than me, got it around her seventeenth birthday. I had terrible headaches. My mother put me in a dark room for days at the time. My dad took me to a doctor. I got some medicine that did help a bit.

My father was a harbor pilot. I sometimes was allowed to come with him on the ships. We went first on a small boat to the big ship.

On one of these trips I saw the sailors with this monkey. He was cute, but funny in a weird way. He would come to me, wiggling and walking like a drunken man. Soon I found out that was really the case. Those sailors were feeding him alcohol! I was so sad and asked my dad and the captain if I could take him home. I promised to take care of him well. To my great pleasure and surprise, they said, "You can take him home." My monkey's name was Keesje.

My dad stopped at a place to get food for him and a small harness with a long rope. I was so happy, fed him at home, and took him to my room. Let him play in my bed, on my furniture. He was so good, wanted to be with me all the time.

The school bus came at six in the morning and took us home again at one o'clock. During that time, Keesje was in my room and he did fine. The rest of the time he was with me and my family. Everybody loved him. We had a big tree in front of the house. I had made a sort of stable place to sit there to study or read my book. Now it was perfect for my Keesje too.

My oldest sister, Fransje, had a baby. Her husband was an engineer on a ship and often gone for months at the time. When their baby, Hansje, got bigger, I was allowed to take him on my bicycle with him in front of me in a little seat and Keesje on my shoulder. That was great.

We lived near the ocean in a protected area for the officers and for the people from the ships who stayed a few days before they went on their way. There was a store I could go to. They had delicious ice *pasra* which is similar to a Slurpee. My brother Jan came often too, but I rode with Hansje and Keesje. Jan was older than me, but I was more careful.

When I was home, Keesje was good; but if he got out to our neighbors, he was bad. There isn't milk in Indonesia like here. We only had condensed milk because of the tropical weather—very hot! We never left anything uncovered, but the neighbors did. They didn't have kids.

Well, my monkey loved sweet things. The minute he saw the jar with that milk, he put his hands in it and licked it and spilled it all over the place. When the neighbor saw that, she yelled so loud that the monkey jumped on her beautiful chandelier, swinging it around. Oh, dear, was she mad. Keesje was so scared that he jumped off it and jumped on her furniture, etc. It was horrible but so funny that I laughed and laughed. Keesje thought it was funny too. He finally jumped into my arms and I took him home.

He was usually with me or on a long rope, but every time he somehow got loose, he ran to the neighbor's house and looked for that condensed milk. I guess he really liked it. My neighbors didn't like me anymore. I got in trouble often.

I really loved Keesje, he was obviously also happy with me. I had him for a little over two years. Then it became too dangerous for us to live there. The young Indonesians wanted us out, made it unsafe for us anywhere. One day they shot at our school bus.

My father immediately made reservations for Mam and us five younger children to go back to Holland. Fransje and her son Hansje came later with her husband. It was 1949 and the Dutch East Indies became officially Indonesia. My dad had to stay two more years to get his pension. He still had five kids and a wife who needed him for support. Pa came home in 1952.

My poor Keesje. I was not allowed to take him with me so I had to leave him with the people who were running the office. They promised to take good care of him, but I never heard from them. My dad had to live in a protected place and never saw him. I felt and still feel so sad about that. But we had two good and happy years together. So, I'm very glad about that. Those were some of the best years I had in Indonesia after WWII. I don't remember much of those very early years. I hope it was good for you too, my dear monkey.

RETURN TO HOLLAND 1949

We returned to Holland on the *Oranje*, a Dutch ship. This was the second time we came to Holland. There was still no room for us to live together. We were all spread out again. Mother was able to stay with the single niece of hers who lived in a one-bedroom apartment in Amsterdam. My older sister Claar moved in with them. Jan went again to Grandpa Zeeman, and Trixie stayed with the family with twelve kids.

Letty and I went stay with Pa's brother in Almelo, far from Amsterdam. *Oom* Jo and *Tante* Miep lived in a small city where the only transportation available was our bicycles. The weather was usually rainy and cold. It took us thirty minutes to ride to school.

Again, they also didn't understand that we weren't used to the Dutch food. Even then, in 1949, the food was scarce, except for bread, potatoes, vegetables, and some fruit. They ate later and had some meat, saved the gravy for us for the next day.

My two cousins, Claar and Beppie, were there too. They were much older than us. Claar had a child, Erika, who was close to Letty's age. My uncle often crossed his arms around us and put his hands on our breasts. He did it to his daughters too, but nobody said anything. Letty and I didn't like that. To them it seemed normal, but we felt weird and didn't dare to say anything.

Letty was so unhappy she cried herself to sleep every night in the first fourteen days. Letty begged my mother to come to get her. Erika always got into the few things that Letty had.

Letty also had to ride the bike to school too. She is two years younger than me and she had polio when she was four years old in the camp. Nobody did anything about it then. Her left leg is still much thinner and more than an inch shorter than her right leg.

When my mother came to visit, I told her that she had to take Letty back with her. Thank God that Mam came and took her away. So, I stayed over two months more—October, November, and part of December in 1949.

School was difficult. I was so far behind in many subjects that I just couldn't do it. I had missed three and a half years of schooling while I was in the war camp in Indonesia. In Holland the kids were bullying me, calling me stupid, and more. I was older than most even though I did several classes in one year to catch up. I knew that I wasn't dumb.

My father sent me to the *Hogere Burgerschool* (HBS), our version of high school. However, in Holland one only goes to high school if you're a good student. If you're less "smart," you have to go to the MULO. The first one prepares you for a higher education and the latter one prepares you for a job when you're finished.

My sister Nel and I in Amsterdam

Anyway, I was behind in just about every subject. The only subjects I was good at were language, math, and physical education. This was simple to understand because I never studied history, social studies, drawing, singing, almost all the fun classes. I came brand new from Indonesia to Holland.

I had to ride on my bicycle for thirty minutes to and from school. I was totally lost. I never had seen or known this family I was now living with. They were total strangers to me and they didn't understand me or like me. No wonder. I wasn't used to their food, drinks, and many other things. I was far from any of my parents and siblings. I can't remember if we had a phone then.

I found a young boy who really liked me and I guess had compassion for me. So, I "fell in love" and we rode home together. It was really nice to have at least one person who liked me then. After a few weeks together, he kissed me. My aunt saw it. She was so angry that he never came around again. I cried.

When I went to Amsterdam for Christmas vacation, I told my mother that I wanted to work and go to school at night. I was only fourteen years old. She didn't like it but understood that I just didn't want to go to a regular school again. After Christmas my mother found a place for all of us to stay. I could come back. It was a store and we made extra rooms.

My father wasn't back in Holland yet. He wanted everyone to go to school and become office workers. My brother Jan had to find a school to learn a trade. My father had already sent my older brother Piet sent to school to become an engineer and get work on the ships.

I was the only member in the family who didn't stay in school until my eighteenth birthday. My father was so angry at me that he didn't speak to me for a year.

For most of the eight years I lived in Holland I worked full time and went to classes three nights a week from six to nine o'clock at night. I got the equivalent of a high school diploma for typing, shorthand, and accounting.

My dad resented that I went to work instead of school. He didn't help me much. He later made up for it. He was very proud when I got the HBS diploma (high school) and certificates for typing, shorthand, and English!

(l-r) Pa and Mam, Oom Jo (my father's brother), Tante Miep, Piet, husband to Rosa, my father's half-sister and my aunt

CHRISTMAS IN HOLLAND

Christmas 1950 my whole family lived in Amsterdam. My father was back for the holidays. We finally got a small apartment on a canal. It had two bedrooms, a small kitchen, living room and a toilet. There wasn't a shower or bath room. My mother put a BIG pot on the stove to warm the water. We all used it to wash ourselves. We went to the bath house to take a good shower once a week. Back then this was normal.

I slept in one bedroom with my three sisters. My parents slept in the living room, my brother Jan in the other bedroom with a partition to separate the room from where my grandmother slept. It all was such a big difference from Surabaya, Indonesia, where we had a big house, big rooms, and big bathrooms. There, we took a shower every day, often twice a day. The food was made by our servant. It was Indonesian food, delicious, with rice, special prepared vegetables, meat, and much fruit.

In Holland we ate potatoes and vegetables and very little meat or fish. My mother was not a good cook. She never cooked in Indonesia because that was done by the servants. She actually liked to cook but that was not allowed then.

On December 5th we saw St. Nicolas and his helpers coming on a boat to Amsterdam's harbor. He looked very impressive with his stately hat and staff. The helpers are always full of soot because they have to go through the chimneys to bring the presents.

St. Nicholas gives the gifts to one of the helpers. They deliver the gifts to the children. Each gift has to have a poem, sometimes sweet, sometime funny and sometimes not so nice if the child was not so good. It's a fun and exciting time.

Then on Christmas Eve, we all go to the special night mass. The next morning, we visit our aunts and uncles and other family members. It's customary for the younger generation to go out and visit the elders. Everywhere we prayed, gave thanks for our life. They had special Dutch treats and drinks. My parents stayed home to cook our special Christmas meal. Most people make something like what we eat here. Turkey, mashed potatoes, vegetables, and pumpkin pie.

When we came home from the visits, my *Tante* Vi and *Oom* Pierre and their two sons, who also had lived in Indonesia most of their life, made together an absolutely delicious Indonesian meal. We ate *gado-gado, sate, krupoek, sajoer boontjes, bali ketjap,* and rice. What a caring and wonderful surprise! We all held hands and sang praising God for everything, for showing us that life is good as long as we have Him to show us the way and have families who love and care.

My friend Loesje (l) and I

My parents let us all in turn thank God for something we really were extra thankful for. That was like a magical time. I never felt so close to God and His care.

Today, in the USA, we celebrate Christmas with a jolly happy Santa Claus and gifts for everybody. In our family, chosen by all, we have a fantastic Indonesian meal, which still gives us a touch of Indonesia. We go to church or just pray at home. It's also a very nice and happy time.

WORKING IN AMSTERDAM

I applied for a minor job in an office to file and later to type. I was only fourteen years old and it was against my father's will that I went to work. He was a captain on a ship, wouldn't be back for a year. However, my mother agreed with me.

I started at Van Amerongen in Amsterdam. I loved it there. My boss, Meneer Gertruden, was such a kind older man, he seemed to understand me. He helped me, often said that I was doing well. I felt useful and appreciated.

My work was simple, filing and some typing. But it was fun. I had the best boss I could ever have. He was kind and made work interesting and fun in spite of its simplicity.

At lunch break we were allowed to play table tennis or bridge. Around two o'clock a "fish farmer" with his cart came by and we ordered fresh "new" herring with some onions on it. We let a basket down with a rope from the third floor with our order and pulled it back up. I loved the herring!! Never ate it before, but I agree the YOUNG herring "raw" is delicious.

I had never done that before. It was so much fun. My boss was always game to do it with us and treated us with kindness. It was the first time in my life in Holland that people were nice to me and my boss understood me, that made me feel accepted.

The first thing I did with "my money" was to buy a good bike. Then I had my teeth done. At that time my mother didn't have much money. The health services were not free and I had thirty-two cavities. It was bad and painful. I found a dentist who filled them all. I paid him from my money.

I rode my bicycle through rain or shine and I liked it. I had a raincoat that covered me good and the ride was fun. Many people got to know me and waved at me and smiled. I worked then ten hours a day and four hours on Saturday. I went to school three nights a week, for three hours each night, for four years.

School was good too. I was with older students and most were nice to me, in spite of my being a bit different and not knowing many simple questions because of my lack of early schooling. I was very eager to learn and that made me accepted by the teachers. I rode my bicycle to school too.

I was very proud of myself and so was my mother. I loved her so much, she really helped me a lot. Mam would wake me up with a cup of tea and a biscuit every morning. When I had my monthly period, she would wake me up thirty minutes earlier because I was dizzy, sometimes fainted, but felt better later on. We all had to do chores in our small place but she often excused me.

I also played bridge with my mother every Friday evening. We were A+ players. I played table tennis in the Dutch club and played many Saturdays all over Holland against other clubs. We were good and I loved it.

Life goes on. A year and a half later I got a job right next door to our apartment on the ground floor. This company made beautiful furniture. I wanted it because we still worked at that time forty-four hours a week. I also went to evening school. I could be home in five minutes. This gave me more time for studying and free time. I also got paid more money. But I really needed the extra time off. I learned a lot of how people in Holland lived, their humor, their likes, and friendship. I finally felt more accepted.

On Saturdays we went to the bath house. Our apartment had no tub for bathing, only a toilet and a small basin to wash our face and brush our teeth. Twice a week, in the kitchen, my mother filled a big basin with warm water for us to wash ourselves. One basin for three people! At the bath house we could wash our hair and have a good bath. I also did homework on Saturdays and I spent some time with my boyfriend.

Sometimes we went to a movie with my mother, and sometimes on Sunday to an early mass. There was dancing organized by our church every Sunday after mass in the winter. Ger and I were good dancers and we were always on the dance floor. In the summer we would go to the *Vinkeveense plassen* (a lake not too far from where we lived) with the family and sail. If the weather was not good for sailing, we went for a long walk in the park. When my father was in Amsterdam, he would sometimes take us to Indonesian restaurants. I was very happy then.

I have visited Amsterdam every time I have returned to Europe. My mother was born there, my parents were married and had their first child there too. No wonder my mother always told us great stories from her life there.

(l-r)Trixie, Me, Letty, Jan, and Claar

MY FATHER'S RETIREMENT

My father had some good years while we were in Indonesia before World War II. We went back to Holland in 1949, but Pa had to stay until 1952 to get his full pension, and then he came and joined us in Amsterdam. It was hard for him. He was only fifty-two years old. He still had six children to raise and get through school. He decided to take a job as a captain for one year on a cargo ship that went to South Africa.

On the return voyage, they stopped in Berlin, Germany, where the sailors got into a fight with the Germans. When he went out to stop the fight, a German stabbed him in the eye with a buckle. He was rushed to the hospital. He lost his eye forever. It all happened very fast, and we were all so sad, but glad he escaped with his life.

My parents, Petrus and Maria

VACATIONS AS A CHILD

In Indonesia, before I was six years old and the war started, we went to a nice hotel in the mountains with ocean views and a swimming pool. I know it was fun, but I don't really remember it.

The next vacation I experienced was when I was almost twelve years old. My parents took us to Tretes on the island of Java, which was a vacation area. This was after the war and before we returned to Holland for good.

It was so much fun. I rode a horse for the first time and loved it. I was with my parents, three sisters and my brother Jan. We all got along very well. We often swam in the pool, played games together and told fantasy stories, or rested under the trees. We all felt the love and camaraderie of a family at peace.

Too bad that it didn't last long. Until my fourteenth birthday we lived on the shore of Surabaya. There were more and more young Indonesian freedom fighters and it became dangerous for the Europeans who still lived there. We stayed a little over two years. Then one day they shot at our school bus. My dad immediately sent us all to Holland. He stayed two more years in Indonesia.

In Holland we didn't have much money and there wasn't enough food anyway. My mother hadn't cooked for us for many, many years. It was a very difficult time for all of us.

One summer in Holland we went on a bicycle trip through the country. There were cities we had never seen. Very rustic and nice. Everywhere we saw flowers—in and on houses and on street corners. We passed many pastures which were green, again flowers in abundance, and water.

We often had to pass streams, ponds, and small lakes. At night we asked the farmer if we could sleep in the hay for a small fee. And they were kind and always let us sleep there. That was when we had vacation in the summer.

When Dad came back from Indonesia, he had brought his sailing boat, and we sailed in that every Sunday, weather permitting. One time, on a short vacation we went in that boat through the canals and locks and finally out to the North Sea, a short distance from the land. It was exciting. Of course, Pa was a captain of the sea. So all went well.

When I got married in 1954, I was still very young. We went to Paris, set our tent up in *Bois de Boulogne*. It wasn't comfortable. The camping ground was clay and hard, but it was very reasonable and close to the city.

My father's boat

Paris is indeed a fabulous city to visit. Great and beautiful buildings and bridges. Fantastic museums of all kinds. We used the Underground mass transit and walked a lot. We even saw a show in one of the fantastic theaters. A few years later we went to Canada and life took a different turn.

MEETING MY HUSBAND

When I was finally able to live with my family in Amsterdam, I had a girlfriend, Loesje. We went out together and found boys our age. We had fun, but I really was into many things much wiser than that, and I soon stopped. I had a job and went to evening school. There was one boy who liked me and came around a lot. He was fine, tall, and handsome. I, for the first time had fun without worrying about school and work. All went well.

The only time I mingled just to have fun was on Sunday after church. They always had a dance all afternoon for the young people. I love dancing and learned a lot of dances.

One day when I was sixteen, my friend Loesje asked if I would go with her to a party for a friend of hers. Her friend, Gerrit Bres, was turning eighteen years old. He was in an orphanage. At that age they gave you a nice party and it was time to move on. He had five sisters and one brother. His mother had died but his father could not care for all of the children by himself, so he kept the two youngest girls and put the others in an orphanage.

Gerrit was going to live with his aunt and get a job in an office. He was six feet tall and, I thought, quite handsome.

We right away hit it off. He took me home and from then on, he picked me up from home and rode me to work on his bicycle, and picked me up to take me home. He took me to evening class three times a week and again took me home. I never saw or was alone with another male friend again.

Even when he went for two years into the service (that was compulsory at that time) we were close. We wrote each other every day and I put a cigarette in the letter every time for him. But we really never were all alone. Even at night when we said good night to each other on the stairs, the door had to be open just a little bit. At age eighteen I was engaged, and when I was almost twenty, we married.

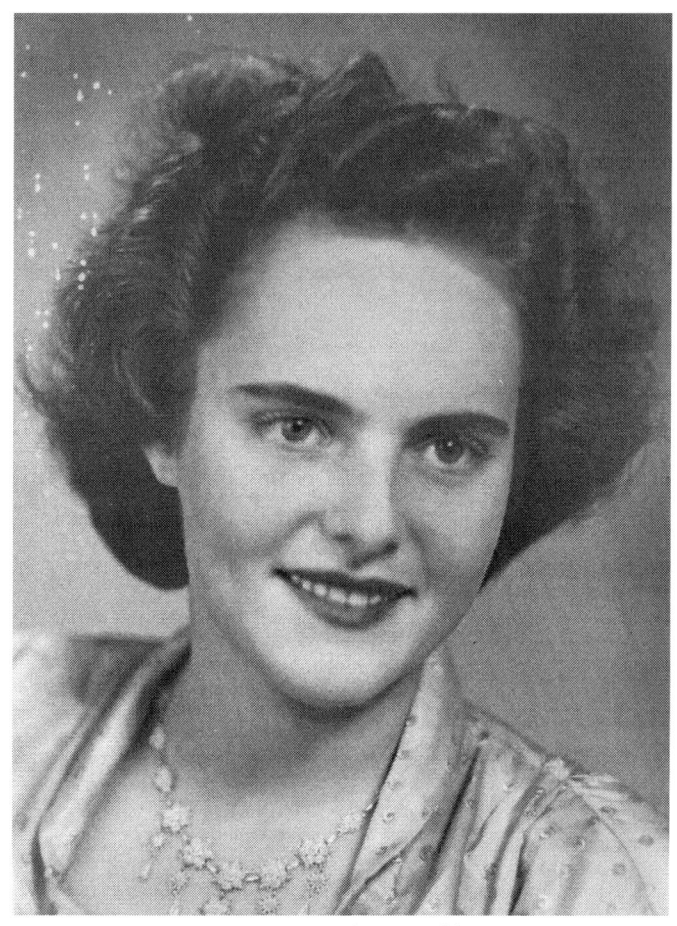

Me as a teenager after World War II

LOVE IN BEAUTIFUL AMSTERDAM

Amsterdam is a beautiful city full of history, architecture, famous painters, and so much more. There I met my first boyfriend. Then I met another tall and handsome young man—Gerrit Bres. I was sixteen years old and Ger was eighteen years old when we fell in love. We did so much together and he rode me on his bicycle everywhere.

I lived in front of one of the canals. Twice one winter the canals froze completely. The schools and many businesses were closed. Oh boy, was that fun. We went skating on the canals. I never did that before, but Ger said, "Oh, that's easy. I help you."

So, I got those wooden skates tightened on my shoes. We did not have boots with blades then. I was shaky on them, but surprisingly I soon got better. We would hold hands with a whole row of teenagers and skate through the canals. It was so much fun.

Later on, I enjoyed going to the many museums. I could spend lots of time there. When I was working for a company close to the *Rijksmuseum*, I had my lunch on the steps with my co-worker and then would spend thirty minutes inside to see the beautiful paintings. It was free for us and I loved the outrageous and famous paintings—from Rembrandt, Van Gogh, and many more! Those were great days.

There's a wonderful opera building. The acoustics are so good. I've seen some wonderful operas and operettas. Once they had Louis Armstrong there. Oh boy, what a difference that was! Normally everyone is quiet and serious, but this time we got wild and loud, and some stood on the chairs! (We saw that on movies from the United States.)

When I was almost twenty, I got married. We had the wedding first in the church. There were so many people. Besides our extended families and friends, many of the churchgoers were there too. They all thought that this marriage was made in heaven, to last forever!! So, did I. Then we went on a boat with the wedding group through the canals of Amsterdam! How fun was that! Then we ended in an entertainment park.

Amsterdam has so much to offer. You can "go to the beach" on top of a grand building. There's sand, water, and beach chairs! Or go down and see a great museum with all kinds of inventions or walk along the canals and see all the boats people live on. You can go to see all the beautiful buildings along the canals, see Ann Frank's apartment, or the fancy boats, big ships, and so much more.

Gerrit and I on our wedding day

I've visited Amsterdam every time I have gone to Europe. My mother was born there and my parents were married and had their first child there. No wonder my mother always told us great stories from her life there.

*Jan and Hilda's wedding,
(l-r) Ina (Piet's wife), Me, Hilda, Jan, Fransje, and Trixie*

MY HONEYMOON

The first time I got married, we didn't have much money. Ger and I decided to go to Paris. We had a Harley-Davidson motorcycle, packed it up with our tent stuff, and stayed ten days in the *Bois de Boulogne*. This was a camping place close to the city. The ground was very hard clay. We only had a sleeping bag and the bare necessities with us. But we were young, strong, and wanted to experience life in France. We didn't need much.

We walked a lot, took the bus or train everywhere. We even saw a show at one of the fantastic theaters. We went to the Eiffel tower, climbed all the stairs as far as we could. We had a fantastic view over the city. We saw the *Arc de Triumph*, walked around, under, and on it. Really a very beautiful piece of art in stone. We walked along the Seine. It was so gorgeous and romantic. Saw the beautiful buildings with all the well-known paintings.

When we were out of money, we worked as dishwashers randomly. The people were kind to visitors and let us do it for a few days. It was great! It gave us a good feeling of the native people.

Me with my Harley-Davidson motorcycle

MARRIED LIFE

There were very few apartments or houses available for the younger married couples because of all the damage from the war, the many soldiers coming back, people moving from Indonesia to Holland, and European countries that were poor and had no work either.

To qualify for an apartment, the ages of the couple, when added together, had to equal at least fifty-one years. I was only twenty and Ger was twenty-two, so this did not work for us.

We finally got an apartment in Almelo, in a rural area, because my brother-in-law Luc worked for an American firm there and they had a job for Ger.

I easily got a job as an accountant that I really enjoyed for a while. But it was often far to bicycle to the farms for which I did the accounting. They would put me in their beautiful sitting rooms with a desk full of papers, bills, and more. I had to straighten it all out and put it in the books. Often these were records for the whole year. It was fun, but the bicycling got to be too much for me.

Then I got a job for a company where I had to type long legal papers. I was a good and fast typist. No errors or white-outs were allowed. They liked me a lot, and I enjoyed the work. The pay was great. We were happy there, but the company where Ger worked went back to the United States. He had a hard time finding a job. We had lived in Almelo over two years.

My dream was always to emigrate to the USA, but at that time we could not. Why? I was born in Indonesia, and according to US law, I was considered Indonesian. Ger agreed to go to Canada with me in 1959. They would accept us.

MOVING TO CANADA

I got a job the day we arrived. My brother Piet was already in Montreal, Canada. He arranged an interview for me at the Bell Telephone Company, where he worked, and another one at the Sun Life Insurance Company in downtown Montreal.

I went to both. Sun Life Insurance hired me on the spot for my determination. My English was fair, so I translated the application in Dutch first and then answered all the questions in English. It took me over two hours. I worked there for eight years and loved it. If the province of Quebec had not changed to almost all French, I would have stayed there. I did type French and English policies but my knowledge and pronunciation of the languages was not very good.

(l-r) Me, Trixie, Mam, Hilda (Jan's wife), Fransje

I also went to evening school, did my high school over in English, and took English literature, French language, public speaking, and speed reading. I bowled with my colleagues and my parents, who had also come to Canada a year after us. I played bridge again with my mother. I was really happy then. By that time, I was married almost nine years and we were still childless.

On our days off together, Gerrit and I both liked to cross the border into the United States—Maine, Vermont, or New York State. We loved the beach. We often went to Maine where there was a beautiful beach. We looked for a quiet place away from people, preferably with no lifeguard. We swam in the ocean for a long time, often going far away. We both were strong swimmers. We loved it.

On one of these outings we felt a strong undercurrent. We tried to swim back, but didn't advance much. At first, we weren't worried, but soon we were tired, and I slowed down. Suddenly I felt my husband next to me, yelling, "SWIM, Maria—SWIM!"

I then realized that I wasn't advancing at all. I tried to go again. He yelled still, "Go—please go, swim! I can't drag you. Swim, go, go!" And I did, again and again, my utmost with him close by, also huffing and puffing.

I thought I couldn't make it but he made me try harder, again and again. All I could think of was to swim. It was very scary, but finally he felt the bottom. He was very tall, six-foot three, and pulled me with him. We were exhausted and promised each other not to go far again. I realized that if he had not been there, I would not have made it.

MY GUARDIAN ANGEL

I always considered myself strong, honest, and basically a good person, and I trusted my husband. But one night I found myself walking on the railroad tracks not too far from where I lived. It was three in the morning. I was walking and walking, farther away, lost in thoughts of despair. What was happening? Where was Ger? Where was anybody I could call? Then I prayed to God. I asked Him for guidance. I was still very religious at that age. Nothing was happening, just tracks going on and on. The few cars that passed by didn't stop. They probably thought, "Oh, there's another lost soul or crazy person. Just go on, don't get involved."

Ger and I had gone out with another couple. Ger took off with the wife and let me stay home with the husband. The husband had always been very nice to me. Unfortunately, he wanted more than friendship.

I knew Ger did it on purpose. I had nobody to tell my feelings of deceit. The husband tried to make love to me, but I could not do it. I left, walked on the railroad tracks, wanted to die. But no train came.

I walked on. Then I got so terribly tired, sat down, right there on the railroad tracks! God what am I doing? I will always trust You, Lord. What am I doing here? Then an angel took me by the hand and took me away from those tracks to a bus stop. There was nobody.

I sat down and thanked God to send me His angel to guide me. Then I thought and thought. I'm here to learn a lesson. God gave me fabulous parents but this I have to do alone. I'm strong, I will take what comes to me, bad and good. I'm not bad. Maybe Ger is. Why did he leave me alone with Jacque? Did he want me to be unfaithful to him? Why did he give me so much wine? I'm dizzy and Jacque started kissing me and more.

Where is my husband? I ran out of my own home and walked and walked, lost. But no more!

I came home about seven in the morning. Ger was making coffee. Had a sly smile on his lips. Asked me if all was OK.

I said, looking him straight in the eyes, "Yes, and, you didn't win." He, "What do you mean?" with that sly smile. "You know," I said, "and you should be ashamed of yourself. I didn't do it."

It was never the same after that because I learned the hard way that I couldn't trust the one I always thought I could, no matter what. I should have left him then, but I really loved the bum. I became a stronger person, I guess God prepared me for what there was to come.

MY FATHER'S DEATH

In 1962 my brother Jan had a duplex on the St. Laurence River. This river is very big, it brings ocean liners into the harbor. My brother lived further down the river where it was quiet. Several houses were built near this river. When my mother and father moved to Canada, they lived on the second floor of Jan's house and they were quite happy there.

Even though Pa's pension was good, he got restless in retirement and wanted to do something worthwhile. Since he lived so near the water, he became a Boy Scout Leader and taught those boys how to sail. This was new for the Scouts and they loved it and so did my father. They all loved him and learned to sail well. He did this for three years.

One evening, he was just relaxing in the apartment when he had a terrible pain in his chest. The doctor was called and he came right away. The prognosis was an upset stomach and gas. He gave my father medication for that. After five minutes, the doctor left, and Pa collapsed in pain. My brother Jan took him to the hospital, where he was diagnosed with congestive heart failure. Open heart surgery wasn't known back then, and all they could do was lessen the pain. He lived for ten more days after that. No one was ever told how serious it was.

I worked then for the Sun Life Insurance Company which was ten minutes from the hospital, and my mother worked in that hospital as a nurse's aide. We visited my father every day at lunch time and after work. The rest of the family came when they could, and Pa was still joking with the nurses until the very end. He really couldn't eat much, but mother gave him sips of orange juice. That is what he wanted.

On that fateful day, I was there around one in the afternoon, and after visiting with him, went back to work. As soon as I walked back in to the office, my boss said I had to turn around and go back. The hospital had called.

When I got back, he had died already and they were wheeling him out. The worst part was that I saw his face, and he looked disappointed. This bothered me for years. He had such a hard life as a young man.

His funeral was impressive, and it was the first one I had ever attended. I had seen many, many dead people in my young life, but never one at a funeral, and never someone I loved so much. The church was full and all the Boy Scouts from his troop made a long line and all raised their hands up when the casket passed. I was so incredibly sad and had a very hard time with it. I thought it was not fair and I questioned my faith. Afterwards, I attended many churches trying to find an answer.

Pa in Canada, 1960, teaching the Boy Scouts how to sail

After Pa's funeral, Mam ended up going back to Holland for eight months. When she returned to Montreal, her entire head of hair had turned grey. We could tell how devastated she was by the loss of her husband. She went back to work at the hospital, and although she still loved it, she was never the same. My father's death changed us all, none of us were ever the same.

MY FIRST BORN

Ger and I had always done everything together, going out often to parties and other things. Every year we went on a fourteen-day elaborate vacation. We both made good money and we just didn't believe in saving that much yet. Two years earlier we had bought a beautiful seven-room, split-level home.

We had been married nine years and I really wanted a child. So Ger and I went to a special doctor. He said nothing was wrong with either one of us, we just had to be not so busy all the time. Keep track of the "right" time. And indeed in 1963 I had my wish and gave birth to a lovely little girl. I was in seventh heaven.

I had a girl, what a joy! I thought that she was beautiful and perfect. She came one month early, was born in the elevator. When I went to the hospital, my "super special doctor" had told me that it would still take a while. It was one in the afternoon. He put me in a waiting room. He also sent my husband and my mother away. saying, "Check in around seven tonight."

Needless to say, he was wrong!! I waited in that room for some time. They even brought me tea and just talked to me. About four in the afternoon I felt her. I thought she was coming, but I had no pains at all. I told the nurse to check me. She said she would soon. "Call when you feel a contraction."

A few minutes later I called again and told her to check me, call my doctor. I felt funny. I had no pains, but I felt so uneasy and weird. So, I asked her again and asked for the RN, please.

It was customary at that time, to shave and disinfect you with iodine. They didn't do anything yet. I got frantic and finally the RN came. With a big sigh and by the grace of God, she checked! All of a sudden, they all came, got me ready for the delivery room.

I was on the second floor, the delivery room was on the tenth floor. They put me on a gurney and raced me to the elevator. I heard them call the doctor. He was angry. They said, "But she had no pains." Just then I got a PAIN. Oh, my God, how awful—it was like my body split in half.

I was back in my mind, seven or so years old, with a tremendous pain in my ear. They were cleaning it but had no medication, no gauze, but cut-up strips of sheets to put in my ear to clean it. It was necessary but it seemed that nobody really cared. It had to be done and I sat in this dark corner all alone, not feeling, just being there.

And then I felt something coming out of my body – I heard them say, "Pant—pant—don't push!" I cried, "I can't. It's coming!" They wheeled me into the delivery room. She was out, still with the embryonic bag all over her. They all worked on her and just let me lay there. I heard nothing, I saw them wipe white stuff off her, wipe her mouth, and suction her and, "Oh God, no sound!!"

I laid there all separated, scared, and alone again, waiting. I thought, "It was necessary, it had to be done." I just was there waiting, and then, there was a faint cry. I was back. I was having a baby! I could feel the emotional release in the room. My "super Doc" only had on gloves and a mask. He finally acknowledged me and said, "All is well, you have a girl."

She was six pounds and two ounces. I thought she was the prettiest thing I had ever seen. Later I had to agree that she really wasn't all that pretty yet. She had no hair on her head, or on her face. She was so skinny and so long, twenty-three inches. But to me she was beautiful, soft, and alive. My little girl was born!

We named her Loretta.

MOTHERHOOD AND MARRIAGE

When Loretta was six months old, disaster struck. Ger was out all the time. My brother told me that he had seen him in the movies kissing a girl. I didn't believe him. How could Ger kiss someone else when he had me!! The more attention I had to pay to my little baby, the more often he left. I was totally unaware that Ger was unhappy, that he was cheating on me.

I was sixteen when Ger and I first met. We fell in love right away. It's a weird feeling. You feel like you're flying in the sky between the clouds and the stars. I felt that way for many years.

Ger studied and converted to the religion that I practiced. I thought that was so good of him. We talked about it many times. He also pledged to me that he loved me so much. I was so happy and trusted him absolutely.

However, after we married, I should have seen his other side. I would always find a reason to explain what he did wrong, so that it looked good for him. I did that for many years, never gave him any thoughts of being not truthful. I was so in love with him. And I was actually happy.

When we first came to Canada, he didn't want to go to church anymore. All the talks we had before about Christianity were all of a sudden taboo. The first time we had a family event he picked a fight with my oldest sister's husband. He knew how much I loved my sister, how important family was for me. Of course, I blamed my brother-in-law.

I was the first one to get a job even though Ger spoke English much better than I did and also spoke French. Soon we bought a car. He drove me to work and picked me up. Even when he got a job, he somehow managed to keep on doing that. We played bridge, I was to play with him only. He knew how much I liked playing with my mother.

My boss was a good bridge player. He asked me to keep the scores, and the next day he would come to my desk and discuss the games with me. I was so flattered. He found out that I liked to play with my mother. So, he told Ger that he would like to play with him. Of course Ger felt honored and accepted. I felt it was nice of Ger to play with my boss. However, it was actually very nice of my boss to play with him, so that I could play with my mother.

When I first got pregnant after nine years of marriage, I lost a lot of blood one day while at work. I was only three months along.

I called Ger and he said, "Go to the restaurant and wait for me, I'll be there soon." I wanted to take a taxi right away to the hospital. "No," he said, "I take you."

This was the first time that I questioned him. Why couldn't I go by myself? I worked full time when I was fourteen years old. Went three times per week to evening school for four years. I never stopped working, even in Canada I always worked. Made more money than him. But he was the boss, had the car, and always told me what to do. I never really cared before because I wanted to be with him as much as I could.

This was the first time that I wanted to do my will because I wanted a child so badly. More than him? I got pregnant the next month already again. I did some things my way. Took it easy, had less sex. Ate healthier. Quit bowling and dancing for a while.

Sure enough, I gave birth to my little girl. She came one month early, and she didn't cry right away. They were frantically working on her, leaving me alone, and I prayed and promised God that I would take care of her.

Please let her live and—there was a little cry! Praise God, thank you. Her father came a few hours later. For the first time I realized that he didn't love me as I loved him. I was his possession not his wife to love and honor. I was sad, but I was strong. With God's help all would be OK.

This was the first time I didn't have to work. We bought the best and most expensive outfits for the baby. I also realized that I didn't really have any good friends just for me. Everything always was around the both of us. I wasn't attracted to anyone else. Ger was my husband, my Everything for many years. I was happy and content with just him.

When my brother Piet told me that he saw Ger in the movie with a girl, I didn't believe him, thought that he was jealous that I was so contented.

Now my life was changed. I had a baby who I totally adored. I learned to do things by myself and was proud of myself. I had my family coming over, made dinners, and showed off my little girl. It was satisfying for me, but it wasn't for Ger. When Loretta was six months old, he just disappeared. He left me with all the bills, the house, and took our car.

THE BREADWINNER

When Ger left me and Loretta, I was devastated. I had never lived alone; now I was not only alone but with an adorable little girl who needed me. None of my family knew what happened, I was so ashamed, felt so hurt that I told nobody.

One day my best friend Willy came by. She noticed that something was wrong. I told her. She offered to let me stay with her and her husband for a while. I did just that. In the following month I told my family and decided to sell the house to Willy and Bob and most of the furniture. I rented a small apartment on Sherbrook Street in the city of Montreal.

It wasn't far from where my mother lived with my sister Trixie, who was also now divorced and had a little boy, Danny, who was a year and a half older than Loretta. After a few months I moved in with them. I got a small amount of money from the Quebec child services department and some unemployment. I used the money I got from the sale of my house and furniture for living expenses.

I did the housekeeping and took care of Trixie's son. We were basically happy there. Twice a week I gave dance lessons at the Arthur Murry studio. That gave me some more money and it was mostly fun. I did it in the evening when my baby was sleeping. My life had changed and I was content.

I never heard from Ger, didn't know where he lived or worked. And to be honest I thought, "I will raise my girl by myself and use the money I've got."

I did just that—until he came back when Loretta was two and a half. I was looking to get a divorce but Ger worked on my loyalty to the church and God. I was sad, but I felt that I had to give it another try. We were OK for a while, got an apartment, and he took over, but I kept close track of the money. He treated me well until Christmas came along.

The day after Christmas I felt sick and said, "I can't believe it, but I think I'm pregnant." Well, that night he took all his clothes and quietly snuck out, never waking me. I didn't see him anymore after that until the divorce in 1969. He sat back in court not saying anything, pretending that he wasn't there. I have never seen Ger since. My second daughter Beatrix was born eight months later.

After that, I was the only breadwinner of our little family. Today all three of my children are good members in society, have great jobs and have their own children. We love each other very much. I think that I was and still am a good breadwinner.

BEATRIX IS BORN

When Beatrix was born in 1966, I was living again with my mother and sister and her son Danny. I stayed home taking care of the children while Trixie worked. My beautiful, brave mother worked for the hospital as a nurse's aide, which she enjoyed. We were happy. After a while I met Radjindra. He was from India. We got close and he liked my girls and my family. We often had fun together and went places. It was again a pleasant time.

Mother, Trixie, Danny, and my family moved together to a nice apartment in Montreal West, close to the school where Danny and Loretta went. My two brothers, Piet and Jan, and my oldest sister Francisca and their families were also living near us in Montreal.

My mother and I with nephew Danny, Loretta, and Beatrix

VACATION IN CANADA

One of our family traditions was to go at least once a year on a vacation. Somewhere nice, relaxing, or somewhere wild and exiting—whatever we needed. I was living in a nice apartment in Montreal West with my two girls, my mother, and my sister Trixie and her son Danny. I stayed home. My sister Trixie worked in an office, my mother worked at Montreal General Hospital.

When the weather was finally nice and warm, I got antsy to get out with my two little girls. I found a farm across the border in the state of New York that rented a room for a very reasonable price with good breakfasts and dinner. That sounded just right for us. I packed my girls, one and three years old, into my car and drove to the farm.

It was rather big, they had many cows, some pigs, chickens and much land where the cows grazed. There was also a little stream of water with small fish and more. The farmer and his wife were like we had seen in books—big and friendly—and made delicious food and cookies. Even tea with a cupcake in the afternoon. It was heaven for us. I had nothing to do then but play around with the girls.

We walked in the grassland, saw the cows being milked. In the late afternoon they all walked to their place in the barn. We walked a lot and we often stepped in (or almost stepped in) cow poop. Then we would yell out *"koeienpoep."* That is the Dutch word for cow poop, and the girls thought that was hilarious.

The kids also liked the chickens, they were allowed to pick up some eggs very carefully which they thought was the absolute best. Beatrix talked already quite well and sang Dutch songs with her sister Loretta. Of course, the farmers and their two kids thought that was soooo cute.

We also went fishing!! I made a stick with a fishing line, a floater, and hook. They put it in the stream, wanted to catch a fish so badly, and were quite patient, sitting real still looking at the floater. Once we caught a frog on the hook. I had to take it off and let it go. They were quite teary about it, but I said that was part of the fishing sport.

I finally got a cup and got some small fish for them. That made them happy. We took it back to our room, kept it a day and then they asked me to put the fish back because they were not happy in the small cup. Of course, I was more than happy to oblige. Oh, and the pigs! The farm had three piglets that were so cute. The girls were allowed to touch them. The big pigs were not so friendly. The girls were kind of scared of them and so was I.

Before we knew it, the week had passed and we had to head back home. It was a great vacation. We often remember it. Even today if I mention *koeienpoep* they laugh and remember how much fun we had on our short vacation that year.

TRAVELING TO CALIFORNIA

I got a divorce in 1969. Ger sat at the back of the court room and didn't speak. The judge granted me the divorce on mental cruelty. I was so hurt and wanted nothing from him.

My money was running out. For the last ten years I had lived in Montreal, Canada. I was pretty happy there until it became a totally French-speaking province. I worked for the Sun Life Insurance Company as a bilingual typist. The company moved to Toronto. So did many English-speaking businesses. Half of my family was in Montreal. My knowledge of the French language wasn't very good, especially the pronunciation.

My younger daughter was almost three and I had to think of a good job, so that I was able to support my children. I only had a few hours in the evening to give dance lessons at the famous Arthur Murray Dance School. Trixie, my sister, had met a very nice French man, Pierre, and was going to get married soon. Mother and I found a nice apartment just for her close to a church, a park, and shops. Many of my siblings in Canada had moved to the Province of Ontario because of the changes in Montreal.

My mother said, "Why don't you try California? I go with you and we make a nice vacation from it."

So, in May of 1969 I decided to go to California where my younger brother Jan then lived with his family. This was the second biggest step in my life and I drove with my two little girls, my mother and a girlfriend, Chess, to California. I was counting on my fairly good education and willingness to work to help me succeed.

I drove my old Chevrolet. Chess would accompany my mother back to Canada when she was ready to go home. We had a great time, spent seventeen days on the road, slept in Motel 6 places, always with a pool. I was the only driver, so we did a lot of sightseeing, because we all needed to rest after six or seven hours of driving.

My dream of living in the USA finally came true. I was going to California.

When we came to my brother Jan's place in Whittier, in Los Angeles County, we could all stay there for a few days. I was so lucky. I got a job as a typist for a temporary agency almost immediately. They paid well. I made enough to raise my daughters and still have time for them, and we were relatively content.

My mother went back to Canada and so did my friend. We could not stay with my brother anymore. We finally found a place where we rented a room in a home where a grandma lived with seven children. It was a big disappointment that we couldn't stay with my brother as he had originally promised. Loretta went to school and Hilda, my brother's wife, picked her up from school. She didn't want to take care of my three-year-old daughter, so Beatrix had to go into childcare.

It was very hard to get an apartment then because we were undocumented, and I was the only one making money and I had two small children. We hated that place with the seven children. That grandmother and those kids were awful, and after six horribly long months, we moved again. I finally found an apartment in Cudahy, because my brother signed the lease for me. At that time, we had to move often, and lived in Whittier, Cudahy, Southgate, and Bell.

THE SCARIEST TIME OF MY LIFE

Soon I found an apartment in Cudahy, found a better job, and again we did well. Until one day when I came to pick up my girls from the daycare. They weren't there! This was an established and licensed place. I felt fine leaving them there while I worked. What happened? Well, Immigration came and took them away!!!

Why wasn't I called if there was a problem or anything wrong? The adults and the other children who were still there were very upset. Apparently, the immigration police had picked them up, taken them to Los Angeles because they were not here legally. You can imagine what a shock that was for me. I had nobody to help me. My brother was at work, his wife couldn't come. She herself had two boys who were born in Canada. Actually, it seemed that she and her boys were also "illegal."

When my brother was transferred from Montreal to California, he had a Green Card. He had signed to be my sponsor if anything went wrong. But apparently this didn't apply to my children. So, I went all alone to the immigration office in Los Angeles. I found them after asking everybody where they were. Well, they were sitting in a room filled with lots of brown men who were handcuffed. My children were in the same cell with them! At least they didn't handcuff my little girls!

They were so scared and clinging to each other. Oh, I was so angry, so upset, made such a scene that they processed me that same evening. I had to take them back to Canada, then try to legally enter the US. I was born in Indonesia and was considered OK to get my Green Card if entering through Mexico. I did that, then took my girls back to Vancouver, Canada, to apply to legally bring them into the USA. It was a terrifying ordeal!

EARTHQUAKE

It started out as an ordinary day. I came home from work and picked up the kids. We swam for an hour, ate our dinner, went to bed. But then, all hell broke out. The ground I stood on was moving, the bunk bed where my two little girls were sleeping banged against the wall.

My older one said, "Mom, Mom, the bed is running and hitting the wall."

"Oh, my love, you're dreaming. I'm here, have no fear, close your eyes and all is well."

But all wasn't well. I heard people running out of the apartment building yelling, "Earthquake!" I opened the door, saw many people outside in their pajamas, some just about naked, looking scared, and totally ridiculous. I'm not sure if I want my girls to see that, besides, it was in the middle of the night!

So, I closed the door and hoped for the best. The next day I found out that indeed we had a rather bad earthquake. It was the 1971 quake. It was a big one. Welcome to California!!!

CHILDHOOD DISEASES

Loretta often got colds, bronchitis, and even pneumonia. She also got chicken pox and the measles in the same year. She missed three months of first grade during out first year in California. I had to stay home with her and take her to the doctor many times. I worked then for Hemphill Spring Co. The owner was a seventy-two-year-old lady and she had so much compassion for me and paid me my full wages.

I found a new doctor, Toma, and he said when Loretta was six, we could take her tonsils out and she would be do better. Soon she did go to the hospital, the procedure was done, and sure enough she wasn't sick all the time anymore. The only sad thing was that my mother went back to Montreal. But I definitely thought I had a better chance to survive here with my girls. The girls went to school, did well, and were happy. I was happy too because of the nice weather, the ease of getting a job, and the people who seemed to like and appreciate us.

These early years in California, I think, were my biggest accomplishment. Alone I have fought to survive and do the best I could for myself and my girls, and later for my son as well. I always trusted in God and in the values in life that my parents thought me. Together we survived and are doing well.

THE DAY WE GOT HAMSTERS

My daughters and I lived in a small apartment in Bell. Loretta was nine and Beatrix was six. I was so happy that I got the house to live in. It was cute with a big covered front porch. The living room was as wide as the porch. There was a small kitchen table with four chairs on the right, a fireplace in the middle against the wall on the left. There was also a small couch and a television on the left. Very cozy.

Me with Beatrix and Loretta

The rest of the house was built like an upside-down U. Left was a hallway where one can pull a double bed out of the wall, a bathroom, and an open area with a double bed. We were happy there.

In the front house lived Mrs. Lee. She rented us the back house. She was a very kind senior citizen. I was keeping an eye on her at night. She watched my girls when they came home from school.

We all loved animals. We already had two cats but the girls saw some hamsters in the store. "Oh, can we have them?" Of course I couldn't say no, so we went home with a pair in a cage. Soon we got a big see-through ball that they could run around the house in. They were really cute. They looked pretty with light brown-beige and white colors, white long whiskers.

The girls had fun with them. Took them out of the cage, were gentle with them. One day Beatrix put one in her dress pocket, and lost it. We looked everywhere, under the house, the bed, and other places. Always afraid our cats would eat them. They never did!! We found the hamsters hunkering in the corner of the living room.

Another day we thought one of the hamsters was getting big and sure enough she gave birth to five cute little hairless hamsters that looked like rats to me. Two days later all the babies were gone. The father hamster ate all the babies!! The girls were devastated, cried, were angry at the father hamster, and let him go.

We never found him again, and it wasn't so much fun anymore. It made them think of the babies and somehow the mother hamster disappeared. I got them a new kitten to make them forget. Then we were all happy again.

Needless to say, we never had hamsters or such animals again. But we found out that it was common knowledge that the male hamster eats the young, that you have to separate them after birth. It was a sad lesson learned.

MY SECOND HONEYMOON

The second time I got married was to an interesting and sexy young man from Colombia, South America, Guillermo Acosta. Guillermo and I had both come to this country almost at the same time. We lived in the same apartment building in Cudahy. I had a one-bedroom apartment on the ground floor.

Guillermo and I

The building had a swimming pool which was always busy, often with many children. The management made a rule that only children with their own parents could swim there from five to six o'clock in the afternoon. There were remarkably fewer people then and I always ran home from work, picked up the girls, and swam at that time. That is where I met Guillermo

He was a nice man and from the start he was always there swimming with us. My girls liked him. We fell madly in love with each other and got married a year later in 1973.

We went to Dana Point on a horse farm, and rode the horses. He rode bareback, I didn't. It was fun. We had a place close to the beach for one week.

The next year we took my girls and my mother on the boat to Catalina Island. We had a very nice time there, went to the top of the mountain with a cart and wagon. My mother went the same way back. The girls, Guillermo, and I went by donkey on a narrow trail. It was exciting and fun. We had a nice hotel for one week. We all had a great time together, we were so happy then.

Our wonderful son Guillermo Alonzo was born in February of 1974. Too bad this marriage didn't last either. We divorced after five years, and we are still good friends today.

Guillermo, third from left next to me; my brother Jan, second from right

EMERGENCY SURGERY

When I came to California in 1969 my health was OK. But a few years later I got pains in my stomach. I tried to medicate myself, ate a lot of watermelon. I was told that would help, and it did sometimes. Then I waited again to have it checked.

When I finally went to the doctor, after about three months of suffering, he said that my gallbladder had to be removed. The date was set for the next week, but I had to pay $5,000 upfront, which I didn't have. I went to the hospital anyway and they started to admit me. Suddenly I felt no more pain and thought maybe I could wait on getting the treatment.

I was very worried about the money. I was now in California with my two girls, a new husband, who was unemployed, and a young son. What if something bad happened? So, I walked out.

I ate more watermelon and prayed for the best. My new husband didn't know what to do. I was self-employed with no medical insurance. I made good money, but not good enough to have $5,000 in one or two months. But we had saved $3,000. So we waited another week. At night I had so much pain that I thought I was going to die.

Guillermo rushed me to the emergency at one o'clock in the morning. A doctor did the emergency operation. I didn't know the doctor, he was quite old. I found out later he was seventy-three years old! I was so sick, they put me in the critical care unit and did an emergency surgery to remove my gallbladder. I had all kinds of tubes to give me fluid, medicine, blood, etc. I was so worried about the kids. They were not allowed to come and see me. I laid there for ten days. Never got up. It was horrible.

But an angel was there! Monica! She was the head of the kitchen in the hospital and she was in my Sovereign House Crystal group, my sales business at the time. I had about ten girls in my group when I was selling crystal. Monica asked the nurses to put me in front of a window. She managed to let my children see me. Loretta was allowed to come in for a few minutes. But I had to promise Monica and the nurses that I would try to get up.

Because I had such a bad infection, the cut was from the middle of my breast to my belly button. It really hurt a lot. After that day I managed to sit up and stand next to my bed, soon walked a bit. One more day they came to the window. I could see them. Loretta came in to talk to me again. My husband came too.

We both were new in California, didn't have any good friends yet who we could trust with the kids. After those first ten days and seeing my family, I finally got better. It could have been much worse. After this I looked for a good job with benefits, and Guillermo finally got a job, too.

BUYING A HOUSE

When I came to California. I got work right away, but it was not enough to save any money. So I started to work for myself in my spare time selling Avon, Mary Kay, Amway. The money really didn't add up to much until I sold Sovereign House Crystal. The company changed later to Princess House. Now I made good money. After a few months I realized that I needed to buy a house. I had three children to support.

I wanted to buy a house because up till now, I had never lived more than a few years or months in the same place. Now I was where I wanted to stay.

Guillermo Alonzo

I didn't want my children to move, start school somewhere else, lose their friends, and more, all the time. I wanted a house so they would go to the same school and get friends in the neighborhood, have a place they could always come back to, if need be, later on.

I bought a house in Norwalk. The house was not as expensive as my first one in Canada. This time I had to do it almost alone. It cost me everything I had in valuables and money. Because of that, I think that it was the most expensive thing I ever bought. My children have lived here until it was time to move out, and have come back again for short times. They still have friends from this time. I'm very happy I did this. I still live here, hope to stay until it's time to see my Maker.

I live alone. Many times, family and friends come over. It's close to schools, freeways, and not too far from the beach or from Los Angeles. My children live not too far away, and I'm content and happy here.

Now I only take short trips, either by boat, plane, or car. At eighty-two years old, I think that's good enough!!

Written 2017

THE POOREST I'VE EVER BEEN

I don't count the years I was in the prisoner of war camp as being poor. There my family wasn't poor. We were forced into the camp and traumatized by the extremely abusive conditions. My father was a good provider before the war as well as afterwards, once we were released from the camp.

When I was in Holland I worked for eight years. In Canada I worked for ten years. I was never poor, just comfortable. Then I went to the US, got a fairly good job, but landed in a self-employed job selling Princess House Crystal. I did very well and bought a house.

Disaster struck, I got sick, couldn't work for a month. I found out that in that time I not only lost my own parties but also lost the girls who worked in my group. I didn't have proper health insurance. I was stuck! Thank goodness I bought the house. It turned out to be my savior!

There wasn't any help from the government because I made good money before and had a house. Then I saw in our local paper that the government offered a training course for respiratory therapy! I thought that it was better to have a steady job with health insurance for my children and me. I applied for it, but again I was denied because I had made a little too much money that year selling crystal. I got a minor job working for a steam cleaning business for six months and quit. Then I applied for the course again. I was accepted and awarded one year of tuition. The course is two years, but I could go at my own speed, and completed it in thirteen months!

In that year I had hardly any income at all. What to do? I paid the mortgage payments from the last little I had saved during the years. I wanted to pay that no matter what.

I bought the house because I didn't want my children to move all the time. All my life before this I moved about every two or three years. I had lived in four countries by then and moved from city to city for a better job, housing, or due to unforeseen problems.

Now, I had a house with a fairly big backyard. I built, with the help of my ex-husband, a chicken coop, bought some chickens and a rooster. Soon I had every day about eight to twelve eggs. Some I sold. I also built a fairly big vegetable garden with lots of tomatoes (many cherry tomatoes that we all ate all day), zucchini, green beans, some carrots, celery, green pepper, and more.

I was too proud to ask for help. Only a friend, who was a Jehovah Witness and lived on my street, saw how I lived and gave me a helping hand now and then. I made and/or repaired my children's clothes. It was the most difficult year as far as money was concerned. We were poor. But we were not hungry. We loved and helped each other. And I completed the course. I was a registered Respiratory Therapist until I retired at age sixty. I still live in the same house and have space enough if any of my children come and want to stay.

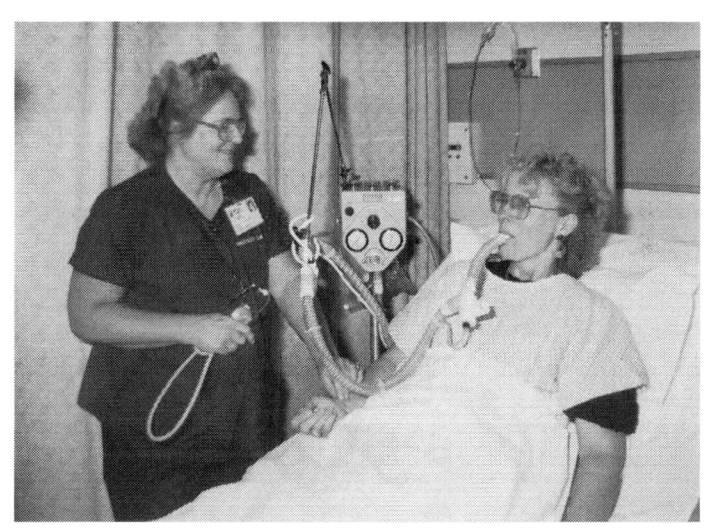

Me with a friend and co-worker who is posing as a patient

CHOOSING MY CHILDREN'S NAMES

My first born! I was so excited, happy, a bit worried too. Yes, we got a lot of suggested names from my baby shower, real nice ones. But I wanted a family name—of course mine and my mother's name which are the same. But my husband wanted a very beautiful name, for a very special girl.

The sitcom starring Loretta Young was very popular then. We loved her name. So, we decided to name her Loretta. No second or third name Ger said, just one beautiful name. So, it was just Loretta.

When my second girl was born, I was separated, so I named her after my sister Beatrix and gave her my second name "Johanna." I was living then with my mother and my sister Beatrix. So her name is Beatrix Johanna.

When my third child was born, I was married to Guillermo, so we named the baby Guillermo. His second name I chose because I liked it with his first name together. It was Alonzo. When he was bigger, he always wished that I had given him my father's name as a second. But Guillermo Petrus doesn't sound good together, that's why we choose Alonzo. So his name is Guillermo Alonzo.

All three names are very different, and so are my children—very different. I did well with the names, I think.

*(l-r) Guillermo, Beatrix, and Loretta, with Loretta's children,
Casey (lower left) and twins Garland and Kenneth*

MY LAST JOB

When I first retired, I did home health care. My first patient was an old lady who had heart surgery and needed help at home. I never did this before, so I had to learn to take care of her and to cook for her. I liked it and she was very appreciative with anything I did for her.

Then I took care of the mother of my daughter's co-worker. She came from a small village in the province of Quebec. Since I lived there for ten years, I knew some of her language and habits. After a few months she became very ill. She didn't want me to call her daughter who was an RN and worked the night shift in a hospital. I mostly held her hand and sang or spoke very softly in Quebec French. I felt that the end was near and as soon as her daughter came home, I told her. She took over and I went home. One hour later she passed away. I was sad, I liked her a lot and I should have called her daughter so that she had more time to comfort her.

Then I took care of a gentleman who was old and couldn't take care of himself. His wife was also old and weak. She had an artificial leg. I really liked them. He was still so in love with his wife and wrote poetry for her and about her. He liked to play Scrabble and she liked to play bridge. I know both games and it was fun, I even subbed for her if one of her girlfriends couldn't play. I was with them about five months and, yes, it was sad when he passed away. I stayed in touch with her, but life goes on.

My next patient was ninety-nine years old and apparently quite rich. I took the night shift from eight in the evening until eight in the morning. She needed twenty-four-hour care. She was a crabby lady and often treated us as servants, which in reality we were. But in this business, it was not smart of her, because she depended on us for everything. Her husband was dead, also her only son. She really had nobody but us, except for her conservator.

I found out that he lived in her house in Beverly Hills. She was living in her own apartment building on the second floor. There were twenty-four apartments. It was not in a good area in

Long Beach. This man came over sometimes and checked what was spent for her food and needs—not paying attention if the items were good, only checking the prices. She actually never left her apartment. Her doctor came to her place. She was weak, couldn't walk, and needed help to go to the bathroom, to dress, and be washed.

We were paid by an outfit controlled by this conservator and he complained that items bought were too expensive. I had never anything to do with that but I got upset that he had the nerve to complain while he was living in her house and obviously taking advantage of her. I reported him to the authorities, but nothing changed. I worked there for almost a year. When it was time to take my vacation, I told them I wouldn't come back. I felt very sorry for her, but I wasn't happy there.

The next gentleman was an old, crabby ex-bigshot who worked in a business many years ago and was retired for some time. His wife passed away. He had no children. But he had a little gray dog that he really loved. He was difficult, didn't like any of the caregivers before me. He wanted me to take him every evening to the same restaurant. The waitress was his late-wife's friend Margie. She was his conservator and took care of his finances.

I came at four o'clock, helped dress him, stayed an hour talking or playing cards, took him to the restaurant, and stayed about an hour. Then I took him home and helped wash him, etc., and also took care of the dog. He was a heart patient but was relatively good. He liked to talk, had almost no friends and no family except a sister in New York and two nieces. But they never phoned or sent any mail. He was quite lonely.

I liked him. He was very worried about what would happen to his dog. I was taking care of them almost a year. It was time for me to visit my mother.

I went to Montreal and arranged to be gone ten to fourteen days. I told him and promised to come back. I also told him not to worry about his dog and promised to take the dog if he would pass away, to make him feel better.

When I came home my son told me to sit down, then told me that he had a call from Margie that Henry had passed away. I immediately got in touch with Margie. She told me that his sister and her two daughters came over and buried him immediately and also his dog.

They took everything and what they couldn't take, they sold. I was so sad and felt guilty that I was too late for his dog. But Margie said they did everything so fast, had the dog euthanized right away. They didn't even want to know how his last days were. I had to write to get paid for my last day of working with him. And that was the end of my care-giving career.

RETURNING TO INDONESIA 1996

My mother lived in Montreal, Canada. In 1993 she gave all eight of her children $5,000 and said, "You can do with it what you want, but I hope that you will use it to visit Indonesia. Visit the place you were born and where we were in the concentration camp under the Japanese regime."

On May 4, 1995, she passed away. She was alert until almost the end. My sister Trixie took care of my mother until she had to go into the hospital. I was there in Canada for my regular visit once a year.

My mother and I played bridge and talked. She was still OK but she knew that the end was coming. After ten days, it was time for me to go back home. The very day I was home Trixie called me and said to come back right away, "Mam's dying soon." I just turned around and took the first plane I could to get back.

When I got to her bed, she looked at me, called me by my nickname, and said, "Oh, Mies, you came back." Six of her children were around her. I held her hand and my oldest sister Fransje held her other hand. About fifteen minutes later she died peacefully.

The following summer, my brother Piet tried to arrange a trip to Indonesia. He and his wife Ina, my sisters Trixie and Letty, Letty's daughter Petra, and I all decided to go. Piet and Ina's very close friends from Holland wanted to go too. So, there were eight of us. My three oldest sisters and my brother Jan couldn't make it.

Everybody left from Amsterdam airport, except me. I left from LAX. It was a five-hour flight to Hawaii and a seventeen-hour flight to Indonesia! Way too long.

I arrived in Medan on the island of Sumatra. When I came off the plane I saw nobody familiar. I found out that the other plane was a few hours late.

Well, what to do? I decided to leave my suitcase and big handbag in a locker and went out. I had to stretch my legs after that long flight! I walked until I saw some small eating places along the road and decided to try something. I was fourteen years old when I left Indonesia for good—forty-six years ago. I soon found out that my knowledge of the official language, a form of Malay, was very poor. Maybe it changed since 1949.

I sat down. They put a small bunch of small bananas (sweet and delicious) before me and I ordered a beer. I was so thirsty. The beer was warm, but OK. Thank goodness that I had changed some of my dollars for rupees, their currency. I was thinking of home in California where they serve chips and salsa!

After two hours, I walked back to the airport. But nobody was there yet!! Now they told me that the plane was coming the next day! What to do?

(l-r) Niece Petra, Letty, Trixie, Me, our hostess, Piet, and wife Ina

I was all alone, spoke very little of their language, and saw no taxis or hotels. There was only the airport, and the unpaved street that I walked on.

But, there was a lady with a sign that had "Maria Zeeman" written on it. Oh, thank you, Lord. That must be for me!

She told me that my brother had called for her to find me and bring me to a place where he had rooms rented. Soon I found out that there were no hotels or motels. Private people would rent out rooms in their homes. She spoke good English, told me what I had to know, and that she would pick up the rest of the family tomorrow.

Meanwhile it was only two o'clock so I told her that I would like to take a *bedja* (man on a bicycle with a big chair in front for passengers to sit in) and go to the *passer* (market). It was an open-air place with food and merchandise.

I asked him to wait for me. I walked through the market that had all kinds of fruit, spices, chickens, and much more. It sure wasn't clean and the market was on sandy ground. I walked further looking for a nicer place to look around.

Would you believe that there was a Mac Donald's? Unreal, but I didn't want to order anything but tea and a cookie. I left soon. But my *bedja* friend was nowhere to be seen. I walked on the street, but hardly anybody was around. My cellphone was worthless here and I didn't see any place that would have a phone. When I finally saw a phone on the end of the street, I realized that I had no small change. Oh dear! It was getting dark. In Indonesia it's dark very fast. And I didn't see a soul!

Then I heard a motorcycle and what do you know, that was the same lady who had picked me up from the plane. I was so glad and she told me that she was looking for me. I had to sit on the back of that thing. It was pitch dark and it was scary to say the least! But she took me back to the place. She told me never to be out in the dark and never say that you're Christian. And don't go all alone, it's dangerous!

So much for the first day in my birth country!!

Our gracious lady who picked me up the previous day was ready to pick up the rest of the family from the airport. When we came back to the guesthouse, we took our rooms and discussed some of our itinerary for the rest of the four weeks we had scheduled.

Everyone was exhausted but nobody would say anything. We decided to see Medan and the surroundings first. We lived there for two years and Letty was born there. The harbor was mostly destroyed, but the house we lived in was still there. We rented a small bus with a driver. Piet still spoke good Malay, but we three youngest in the family did not speak it very much. I still spoke a little bit more. I was six when we went to the camp and hadn't yet gone to a school.

And of course, few people in Medan spoke Dutch or English. But they were very kind and helpful and eager to learn from us. I really felt a kinship of a kind. There were no beggars anywhere. Some of the kids or young people sold hard boiled eggs or sang Dutch songs for us for some candy.

We visited a rubber and cacao plantation. Young teenagers would drive around on their bikes and catch the rubber in a medium-sized can that was tied to the tree and then pour it in their own container. It was amazing how much rubber they collected. There were many, many trees. But they drove around leisurely and did their job, often stopping to talk to us and show their wares.

From there we went to the "monkey mountain." Everywhere you see monkeys, somewhat tame, and many wild ones, in the trees, on the road, everywhere. When we came to the mountain, we told everybody to leave everything in the car that the monkeys might take. But, Ina, my brother's wife, automatically took her purse and a big bag of *rambutan* (fruit) out, even a bottle of water. She lost it all before we could take it away from her.

Thank goodness her purse didn't have her wallet in it. But the monkeys emptied the whole purse and sniffed and investigated what was in it and then threw the purse in the air for fun (I guess).

The monkeys ran around trying to eat the *rambutan* they stole before the other monkeys could steal it away from them. Their actions were really hilarious. Even with the bottle of water. They tried to drink from it while others tried to get it away from whoever had it.

We went back in the car and drove the rest of the way. It was a beautiful scenic road, many more monkeys and trees, and much greenery. Then we found a home where we could rest just before Samosir, near Lake Toba. Very nice place with flowers abounding, kind of on a hill. We had dinner: *lode* (pressed sweet rice), *telor* (egg), *sate* with hot sauce and warm beer, *pisang baranggan, nasi* (rice) *bami* or *goreng.* We also had fruit, then coffee with condensed sweet milk, and, always, small sweet bananas.

Unfortunately, Martin, the friend of Piet and Ina, had a mild stroke. A doctor from somewhat far away came and stayed with him until the morning. Then he told us that Martin should not go any farther with us. So they stayed with a friend of Letty's who lived in Lombok. We caught up with him and his wife Wil three weeks later.

We continued our trip to the Batak area. The people are very friendly. It's very scenic and Lake Toba is so interesting and very pretty. We visited a small village and saw the Batak style houses with the interesting roofs. There are also small houses for the dead. The ground is not solid, so they bury their dead above the ground.

We arrived on a celebration day. Water buffalos are the most important animals on the island of Sumatra. The community did a ceremonial dance, in colorful outfits, to honor them. Later there was a dance with one animal in front. All of us, and more of the natives, wanted to participate. It was fun and interesting.

Then they did a friendship dance and a *Lima Serangkai* dance of love. All in beautiful, colorful clothing. It was so interesting and adoring. The whole trip was worth this experience!!

At this point we started to love the country. We started to notice how close we were to the natives. We weren't scared. We loved them, and we picked up some more words in Malay. We were so glad to have taken up this adventure.

Then we stopped at Sidempuan, a small village, and got a room. It was Letty's birthday. We had a nice dinner, made by Piet, and Letty cut the *durian* (soursop fruit). It was delicious Indonesian food, fruit, and warm beer—like "old times." We sat together with a sweet kind of cake and played our favorite game of bridge.

Later on our trip, we went to the island of Java. One day we visited the Buddha statue at the Borobudur Temple. It is a monument from the eighth century. It was very impressive. We had to walk over two hundred steps to the top. Everything was made of stone around us and Buddha was on the top. We could reach out and touch the foot of him for good luck. Buddhists are very peaceful people; they don't talk much but are always friendly.

The Island of Java

Then we visited Bandung on Java where my dad and my brother Piet were held in the Japanese concentration camp. We had a place to stay for two days. The people were very kind to us. The lady from the place wanted to have pictures from all of us. She showed us a big flower that only blooms once a year for an hour and a half and her flowering banana trees.

We went to the *passer* (market place) and bought lots of spices and fruit. Everybody came out of their stalls and looked at us. They wanted to talk to us and asked many questions. And of course, with the way we were dressed, we were as much an attraction to them as they were for us.

We got on our bus early in the morning and drove through the mountains. That was also interesting and beautiful. We saw a man with a big monkey and stopped for a drink. We gave the man a quarter and his monkey climbed into a high coconut tree and threw a coconut down. We all got a coconut and thanked the man and the monkey!

We saw some native ladies, gave them a quarter, and they cut a hole into the coconut big enough for us to drink the juice and eat the flesh of the fruit. It was delicious! We came to an open wooden building where many colorfully dressed children gave a show. They also made music with a wooden instrument.

Then we went to Tretes. We used to go there on vacation before the war, and once, in 1947, after the war. It is more modern now. It had nature baths—big, like a swimming pool—circled by beautiful bougainvillea and other trees and bushes. All the land around there is used for rice and sugar plants.

Our next visit was to a primitive village. Here we had to go down five hundred and eighty steps. Very exhausting for us. But it was interesting. The village is totally self-sufficient. They ate vegetables, rice, fish, and some chicken. There were banana and other fruit trees around. No cars or bicycles. The small houses were from wood with straw roofs. Space between the houses was only about five feet. There was a small pond with fish, which provided the main dish for our meal.

But, when I had to use the bathroom, I found out they used the pond for that. They cooked with that water and used it for drinks. They were very kind and it seemed that everybody was happy. They all helped each other. They also washed their cloths in that pond! Needless to say, we didn't want anything to eat or drink after that!!

We also went to Jakarta's harbor. We looked at the homes we lived in. I didn't recognize them, but Piet did. The harbor looked so unkempt and dirty. We drove in a small bus with a driver to where we were in the camp. We all remembered "Ampasit E" (the street name) and the house!

It was rebuilt, but the street looked the same. We stood in front of it. The lady who lived there came out. I think that she understood why we were there. One doesn't see many European people there.

She spoke Dutch and asked us to come in, but we didn't want to. We were happy she talked to us. The house looked very nice, we told her.

She said, "Yes, I changed everything in the front and in the house. We all try to forget." We left here in 1945, fifty years ago. This was the first time we came back. We were glad that we did. We were able to put some things behind us. Life goes on.

We still had to visit Surabaya. We had gone to Holland for seven months, then returned to Indonesia and lived in Surabaya until we returned to Holland again in August 1949.

We left Jakarta by boat. It was a *praw*, an open boat used to transport not only people but also chickens, pigs, and more items to sell. We sat on a bench between the natives. It was quite an experience! But we made it safely. They all were accommodating and kind.

The first thing we did, arriving in Surabaya, was to hire a car and driver and try to go and see where we used to live. Unfortunately, it was now all a military base. We were not allowed to enter this area.

The office building in Surabaya where my father worked

The house we used to live in was on the other side of the building and offices for the harbor pilots. There was a waterway between this and our "ex-house."

We drove around to that place and could look at the office and tower where my father used to work. Piet still spoke fairly good Malay and they let us go in, look around the area, and go up to the tower where one could see the ships come in. Always in the company of some guards. But they were friendly and sort of excited with our visit. Some of the writing on and in the building was still in Dutch.

Then we went to the school we attended for almost two years. But we couldn't go inside. We stayed again in the guestroom of a very nice lady's house.

We were glad to have seen our house, my dad's ex-office and surroundings, and try to put it all behind us. Indonesia is a beautiful country. The people were very pleasant, helpful, and nice to us.

We were glad because it was our birth country. We were very happy here except for the years the Japanese tried to take it away for themselves. The Indonesians seem OK on their own now. I hope they're all happy and content.

We, the family Zeeman, are all spread out now in the Netherlands, Canada, and the USA. We always have kept in contact with each other, no matter where we ended up. This trip was a closure for all who came along on this trip. And for all those who couldn't come, we shared our experiences with them.

NEVER TOO OLD TO LEARN

As a little girl, I was in a concentration camp under the Japanese regime when Japan occupied Indonesia during World War II. During the many years that have passed since then, I learned to forget and to go on. I had several friends who were Japanese, but I would never buy anything that was made in Japan. Once I even chose not to accept a better job when I found out that my supervisor was Japanese. It made me think of long past, sad times. I must say that most all my life I was too busy having a good time to spoil it by thinking about the camp.

I always worked hard and studied hard, wanted to be the best mother I could. I really never took time out for just me, my inner self. Then I retired, earlier than I wanted. Again, my time went for extra work to make money for the care of my children and grandchildren.

I still carried a grudge that I was hurt, not only by the Japanese, but also by the Dutch people, because when we came to Holland, hardly anyone was nice to us.

I know that they went through a war too, but they weren't skinny and hungry. A Dutch organization gave us double coupons to obtain food. Others were envious of that. And, of course, we spoke Dutch, but with no dialect. They thought we had our noses in the air.

In school they laughed and teased us because we were far behind in every subject. I was nine years and had to do grades one, two, and three in one year. No wonder I was still undereducated for my age. I made up for it for many years to come. The older we get the more we learn and understand.

Then one day, in 2003, a lady from the Netherlands came to my home in Norwalk. She spoke Dutch to me and said she was looking for any survivors of the Tjideng camp in Jakarta during World War II. I am one of them. They had been looking for me for years.

She talked to me for a long time. Then she offered me a visit with a psychiatrist, but his office was far from me. I had often thought of my life, but hardly ever talked about it.

I talked with my regular doctor and he referred me to a different psychiatrist. But when I explained my situation and my life, this psychiatrist told me that he had never heard of the war in Indonesia during World War II.

I was dumbfounded and kind of upset. I thought doctors were so smart and well educated. Later I found out that many people in the United States didn't know that Indonesia was invaded and occupied during World War II, from 1942 to 1945.

I went back to my doctor. He referred me to a counselor, Alma Smith. She also didn't know anything about this war, but she said, "I'll read up on it before I make an appointment with you."

She was educated in Mexico. I liked her and I agreed. I had many sessions with her. My daughter Loretta had been encouraging me to join a writing class. Alma also recommended that I join a writing group.

I saw Alma for eight years. She was very understanding and helped me a lot. Unfortunately, she left. I still had to see another physiatrist, but just for some medication. This Dutch organization gives me some money (restitution) for the rest of my life. I'm grateful for that and grateful that I can talk about this sometimes.

Now I'm a senior, and in this writing class. I listen to the other people in the class. I learn and take time to understand other people, how different they are. I talk to other people more freely now.

Here, I had another big change in my life. I met a Japanese lady from California named Kay. I was still very much against anything to do with Japan, but she was such an inspiration to me. She was very thankful to be here in the United States, wrote such insightful stories that I realized that it was dumb and not righteous to deny everything that was Japanese.

Kay also had a war experience somewhat similar to mine, but without the brutality. She and part of her family in California were forced to live in the Japanese internment camps during the war. They had adequate food and medical services, but people lost their homes and property during this time.

When I listen to Kay, she makes me think of her. She thinks of other people from a very wise and humble standpoint. I finally felt that I could love her for what she is, Japanese or not. I felt such a burden of relief falling off me that I was quiet and thankful. When we left, I saw her outside, I called her and hugged her, thanking her for being Kay, wise and understanding. Yes, even at eighty-two years old one can still learn a lot in life.

(l-r) Kay Okino, Me, and Loretta

I was in a war and that changes people. The Japanese soldiers were very mean and cruel. But if someone else had taken our land, they would probably have been so, too. Just look what happened in Germany and in Europe!

I'm now at peace with the Japanese people and the world. I feel so much better. Not with the leaders who start wars, but with the world as a whole. My children and grandchildren visit me often and love and respect me. That makes me happy.

Written 2017

REFLECTIONS ON INDONESIA

Many things happen in a lifetime of eighty-one years. My mother was an educated woman, but, in my opinion, she was very naive about people and her beliefs and sex. When I was in the camp, she always sang songs of praise and love to God. But she couldn't explain to us why those soldiers were so mean, hated us.

"Why?" we asked.

All that was said was, "We're in a war and they don't like us." Later on, I understood that it wasn't particular to us, but that they wanted the land and riches.

The Japanese soldiers weren't taught to love their neighbor, but to hurt and kill us because their emperor said so. They were trained to do so. At that time, they were trained to be happy to kill. Also, it was an honor to die for their emperor. That's unheard of with us. We were taught to love each other and not to want what others have.

But the Dutch companies took Indonesia and called it the Dutch East Indies, ruled it for three hundred years.

What the Dutch companies didn't do was to teach the native people how to take care of their land. The Dutch people were already far advanced in technology to do that. They made big plantations with good machinery and had the knowledge of how to take care of the land.

They also had the knowledge to bring the big ships in to most of the larger islands. In other words, they were far advanced in just about everything to make it a rich and good place to live. The Dutch wanted to rule it forever, and have the riches sent to Holland.

The Dutch companies took care of the native people, but kept them uneducated and just happy to be able to eat and have the things they needed. But they didn't send the native people to school or teach them our language. We learned theirs, so we could control them. I agree that wasn't right.

Many of the native people fought with us against the Japanese regime. We had not much of an army, so the Japanese took over soon.

The native people were not interned, but not taken care of either. If they didn't do what was expected, the Japanese were very cruel to them too. By the end of the war the Japanese soldiers told many native young men to fight the Dutch to get their country back. Well, they did get it back.

In 1949 Sukarno came in as a new leader and The Dutch East Indies changed to Indonesia. The young Indonesians were then against all people who were not natives. Most non-natives left to other countries.

Written 2016

SHARING MY STORY ON STAGE

On March 11, 2018, I was invited by the KPCC In Person series, Unheard LA, to share my story on stage in front of hundreds of people. At this time in my life, I am honored to be chosen and to have the chance to speak about my life to so many folks who have never heard of me, or of the Japanese concentration camps that took place in Indonesia during World War II.

Me with Beatrix (l) and Loretta

This was my speech:

The war in Indonesia with Japan began in 1941. We lived in Jakarta near my father's work near the harbor. The Japanese soldiers stormed in. They moved us immediately to the city and took my father away. The rest of my family moved into a small house. We could still cook for the first few months. Once a week we were allowed to buy food. Our problem was that we had nothing.

I remember my oldest sister, Fransje, asked my mother what she had missed the most durng World War I. My mother said, "Soap." Fransje had worked before the war and had some money. She knew Ma San Jaw, a man who was free. She asked him to get her soap, and started to sell the soap around. We all helped, so we were able to buy some food those first few months.

Then all of a sudden, the soldiers put a double fence around the place and patrolled it. Fransje could never thank Ma San Jaw for helping us, so she threw a thank you note over the gates.

One day, Fransje and four other women were caught trying to communicate with outsiders. They came back beaten black and blue all over. Another morning we all had to come forward and give the soldiers our money and valuables. They were very rough.

It was awful and very degrading.

We were now not allowed to cook or have running water. Every day we went to the big building and received a handful of food. In the morning we got a slice of bread which was like leather, but we could chew on it for a long time.

Twice a day we had to stand in rows of ten people deep. There was about a foot between each row. Soldiers would walk down each row. We had to listen to Captain Missohara, who stood high on a pedestal commanding us to bow down and then stand up. But when Captain Sonei took over, it was very bad. He would make us stay bent over for a long time. If anyone fell, they got hit. When my brother Piet was twelve, they took him away. Other families were put into our house with us. We had a bed and two big wooden cases for our family to lay or sit on.

My mother, Fransje, Nel, and Claar slept on the bed. Jan, Letty, Trix, and I slept on those cases. We got one pail of water a day to wash ourselves. Nel's job was to carry heavy things for the soldiers and clean the small ditches that ran in front of the houses. Everybody had to use these ditches to pee or poo in, or to throw up. It always stank so bad.

Claar had to clean the big black drums where they cooked the food in. Sometimes she would bring scraps of food back to us under her toes. We, the four little ones, did nothing. We had no school, no church, nothing. Slowly we all ran out of clothes and shoes. But we always had soap, and we all played bridge.

My mother and I got sick with tropical sores during the last months. Then, one day we heard the soldiers leave! The war was over! I was nine. We had been living in this camp for over three years. Fransje got hold of a banana and I will never forget how she fed it to our mother with a tiny spoon. We were all so hungry, but Fransje gave the whole banana to our mother to save her life. And it did.

Later, packages were thrown from the American planes. Boxes filled with food, cans, candies, lipstick, and cigarettes. These last two things I had never even seen before. We tried to eat the lipstick! Ma Son Jaw found us and took my mother, Jan, Letty, and Trix on a train to Bandung where my father and brother were. The others had to stay with me until I got better. Two months later, I was better and we, too, went to Bandung.

I had not seen my father or Piet, in four years. I did not even recognize them. My father had awful scars on every inch of his body. He had a huge swollen nose and a long, scraggly gray beard. I did not recognize him.

The violence didn't end with the war. In 1946, we got on the first ship from Indonesia to Holland. Then we all decided to forget the "camp time," never, ever, to talk or think about it.

My wish as a newly-freed nine-year-old, as I watched the American planes give food to my starving family, was, to become an American. In 1969, I came to the USA. In 1974 I bought my house in Norwalk. In 1978 I became a US citizen. I'm happy.

In 2003, a lady came to me from Holland. She was looking for any survivors of the Tjideng camp. We talked for hours and I started to realize that I had PTSD. She advised me to get help. My doctor sent me to Alma Smith, the best counselor there is. She said to join a group to meet people.

I went to a community senior center and joined a writing class, run by Bonnie Mansell. I listened and absorbed. I love to write, but I never before wrote about ME. Always about my travels, family, animals, plants, and more. Now I listened to stories from the people in the class, stories about real life. I want to know why we're here, to accept what was dealt to me and understand the meaning of it. I believe that this community, the writing class, Bonnie, and Alma taught me about myself. I am ever so grateful.

FAMILY

HAVING MANY SIBLINGS

My parents wanted many children when they got married. We were all welcome and appreciated. My oldest sister is very sweet and kind. She was like a second mother for all of us because my mother was often pregnant. There was some rivalry between my two oldest sisters. They got along well but it was always Fransje we went to for anything if mother was not available.

Francisca was the one to read books to us in the camp when we had no school; she would teach us letters and numbers. The last two years when we were in the concentration camp, she was especially nice and good to me because I had more medical problems. My mother spent more time with my two younger sisters. Trixie was the baby and Letty had polio.

My brother Jan and I were only thirteen months apart, so we were always together. We had the least amount of attention, I always thought. Especially my brother Jan.

My dad sent our oldest brother Piet to Holland right after the war to attend college. We didn't see him very much. When I was married and moved to Montreal, Canada, Piet and his wife were my best friends. Nelly, the second oldest, left us soon after the camp time. She was helping the wounded soldiers in Jakarta, Indonesia. After that she got married. Claar was often too old for us. In the camp she had to work in the kitchens. Nel worked also.

In the camp we did really nothing but roam around and sit around. The last two years I couldn't do much because of the tropical abscess on my leg and other medical problems.

My parents played bridge (a rather complicated card game) ever since I can remember. In the camp we played too. Only Claar didn't want too, and I played with my mother, Francisca, and Nel. During the day I played with Jan, Letty, and Trix. Then we just played as we wanted to. It was not good bridge, but it gave us something to do. We felt good about it.

Later I always thought that those games helped us through those years of hunger and pain. And the soft singing of my mother. She had such a sweet, shushing voice. We always had a special bond together. Later on, when we all got married and moved to different parts of the world, we kept in touch. As I write this book, only three of us remain.

Francisca married the young man she meet in Indonesia after the war. They eventually moved to Canada. She is ninety-five years old now.

Petronella was a nurse in Indonesia after the war. She married a captain in the service and had three children. She passed away about three years ago.

Piet married a girl in Holland. They also moved to Canada and he worked for Bell Telephone. Piet has also passed away.

Claar married a man from Switzerland and they lived in Vancouver. She died two years ago.

Jan and his wife eventually made their home in southern California. He passed away.

Trixie and her husband Ralph lived in Montreal. She passed away earlier this year.

Letty still lives in Holland and she visited me earlier this year.

I always felt privileged to have grown up with many siblings. I am grateful to both my parents to have provided me with this wonderful family.

Written 2019

IN HONOR OF OUR PARENTS

Here we are, the "three little ones" as we were called so many years ago. Mother told us to be strong, honest and love your family. Dad taught us to believe in ourselves and "never be a burden to the country you live in." And always honor your heritage.

Well, we came through the camp time. We all three got divorced and came through it OK. We ended up in three different countries. We followed our parents' principles with our children and grandchildren. They all are good citizens, have good jobs, and love the family. We also love and take care of our animals as they did and taught us. And here we are in 2013.

Me—living in my own house with my pets Honey, Lucas, Hero, and Birthday in Norwalk, California, a US citizen.

Letty—living in her own house with Rakkertje, her dog, in Castricum, Holland, a Dutch citizen.

Trix—living in her own house with Mustache, her dog, in Lachine, Quebec, Canada, a Canadian citizen.

We love and honor the countries we live in, yet we'll always be "Dutch" in our hearts. We're happy, content, and respectful with the lives we have chosen for ourselves. We're still very close in spirit and mind. We see each other every one or two years, sometimes more. I was in Canada and so was Letty last October, visiting our siblings. This year my grandson Garland is getting married. My sisters both are coming to celebrate with us.

Written 2013

OUR 1981 REUNION

Our time in the prisoner of war camp during World War II was horrible. We depended more than ever on each other. And yes, by a miracle, we all survived this ordeal, but we never talked about it. It was a rule between us, "It happened, it's over, we let it go." And we did it. We spread all over, Holland, Canada, and the United States. My father and mother lived in Canada for the last of their years. Pa passed away in 1962.

My mother

In 1981 we decided to have a reunion with all of the family on my mother's birthday, including her many grandchildren and others belonging to the family. It was held in the Laurentians in the province of Quebec. My mother lived there and so did several of her children. Trixie and her husband Pierre organized it. We all chipped in our share. They had a big house with many bedrooms, a giant living room, kitchen, and several bathrooms. It was right in front of a beautiful lake. They had lots of chairs and more! It was wonderful.

My mother had asked that each family member would perform a song, or act out a play, or do anything they wanted to on her special day. We did that as kids at every birthday and/or any occasion for our parents. Needless to say, it was wonderful to be with all of our extended family together. Some of the younger ones I had never met. I was there with my two daughters, my son, and grandson. On the day of my mother's birthday we performed.

Each of my mother's children did something about the camp. We listened to each other and realized how much those miserable three and a half years had formed our lives. We also realized that we should talk about it. Maybe not with each other, but with a professional. And some of us did it soon after this reunion, and some, like me, did it much later.

My mother and I

My mother used to dress us three "little" ones (Letty, Trix, and me) the same. We each made the same dress for this occasion, too, and sang the songs my mother always sang to us. She was very touched with all of us and we decided to do it every five years from then on, at different places and having a different family to organize it. She was so happy and touched and so were we. I was sure that our dad looked down at us being very happy too.

MY BROTHER JAN

His name is Johannes, Jan for short. He was named after my father's brother. We didn't know my uncle and heard very little about him. Jan was born in Indonesia, thirteen months before me, and was very ill for the first few months of his life. I came so soon after his birth that I had to share all the attention with him. When he came home my mother spent a lot of time with him. Fransje, my oldest sister, or our nanny took care of me.

But we became "best friends" right away. We played together all the time and were close. Especially when we were in the camp during the war. We didn't go to school, church, or anywhere else. In the beginning we played outside, but soon we were always in the house.

My mother played the card game bridge. My two oldest sisters played. Claar, who was five years older than me, had to learn it too, but she didn't like it and didn't play well. My mother taught my brother Jan, my two younger sisters, and me too. I caught on to the game fast, and when Claar refused to play, I had to step in. I liked it and became pretty good.

Often, I played with Jan, Letty, and Trixie. Even though they were too young to play the game, one has no idea how fast they learned to play the game.

We all knew at that time that we had to be nice to everybody. Times were bad enough. We were all lethargic and slow. Jan was a thumb-sucker all through the camp years. Nobody said anything.

Sometimes he would say, "Well, girls," (while sucking his thumb), "it's not bridge with talking." We all broke out laughing.

Jan didn't look like me but he liked the same games and jokes. When we were teenagers we often went dancing or saw a movie together.

When I was fourteen and we lived in Amsterdam, Jan and I often went out together to dances, played sports, or did other fun things. I was working then and he went to school. We didn't have many friends. We were too "old," too different from many of the children our age because of our war experiences, and too inexperienced for playing outside. I'm so glad that we had that support from each other

We often took the place of each other's boy or girl friend when they couldn't go. I had a boyfriend, Ger, already when I was sixteen. He was eighteen. He went for two years in the army. This was compulsory for all young men. He was far from Amsterdam where we lived. Ger didn't want me to go with other boys. I was also not allowed to go without my brother as a chaperon by my parents. We both were happy with the arrangement.

My brother Jan

Jan and I only grew apart when he left for Canada. I got married and stayed in Holland. When I moved to Montreal a few years later, it was never the same. Jan and I both saw each other regularly, but had different interests.

Jan got married, had two sons, moved to California with the company he worked for in Montreal. Unfortunately, his wife never got used to me, never really understood. We were two worlds apart from each other in about every subject. However, we always came together with our families on holidays, birthdays, and Christmas Eve. My nephews and my family keep the tradition alive, so we still see each other regularly.

I always loved and had a special place in my heart for my brother. I was so very sad, when his wife passed away. Jan died a few years later. He never got over her death. He left so many people behind who loved him.

But because of his marriage and my divorce, we never got close again. I think it hurt us both, we could never make it work again. He was a good person and very loyal to his wife and family. When his wife Hilda passed away, he started to drink more alcohol. That changed him. He passed away at the age of seventy-four years. I always wondered if I could have done something to make him a happier person.

Me with Jan (l) and Piet at a family wedding.

MY BROTHER PIET

His name is Piet. He was the third child in the family. He was special to everybody, especially to my dad. He even looked like my dad, but he had a different personality. I guess more like my mother. More carefree than my dad. More fun, like my mother.

He also was a teaser. One day my oldest sister had a beautiful white dress on. He did admire her, but put a black hand spot on the back of her dress. She only noticed it when she came home. Oh, was she mad at him and embarrassed because she went to a dance party.

When he was a young boy (I heard this story often) he went to a Roman Catholic school where he was intrigued by the nuns. They dressed in long white gowns, had a sort of head covering. Well, one morning he walked behind one of them and lifted her dress up. He wanted to see if they had legs or magic feet.

Oh boy, was he punished for doing that, but everybody else was silently laughing. He grew up a teaser, but always for fun. I loved my brother. If we had any problem in school or anywhere else, we told him, and he sure took care of it! Nobody pestered his five younger siblings! The two older ones could take care of themselves, or they called my dad.

One time, years later, we were all at Lake Thomas on one of our family reunions. We were all in a round hot water tub (sort of a Jacuzzi from wood). He would tell everybody who came near that we were making soup!

He grew up to be a good husband with five boys and one girl. They all loved him a lot. He was well liked at work and all kinds of gatherings. I was so sad when he passed away from a stroke several years ago.

MY SISTER LETTY

I recently went to visit my three sisters in the Netherlands. My youngest sister, Trix, lives in Montreal, Canada. My two sisters, Letty and Nel, live in the Netherlands and my oldest sister, Francisca, lives in Canada, but at the ripe old age of ninety-two, she is unable to travel anymore.

It took me ten hours without stops to land in Schiphol, Amsterdam. It wasn't an easy flight, but I forgot all about my discomfort as soon as I saw Letty. She has always been an inspiration to me. She is only two years younger than I am, so I have always felt close to her.

Letty and I

During World War II, when we were in the Japanese prison camp, she had polio. During the almost four years of camp time, there wasn't anything we could do for it. She was only seven years old when we were freed, and not long after that she got a special shoe with a brace. Her disability was more noticeable with the brace. She not only walked with a limp, but also with a loud sound as her clunky shoe hit the ground with every step. Children teased her often, and she could only play sports or games with other kids if we (her siblings) played with her.

My sister Letty had a hard time, but one day she got sick of it and threw the shoe and brace in the ocean! She refused to ever wear another one, no matter what my parents did. Her leg was much thinner and shorter than the other one. She always walked on her tippy toes with that foot. She was quite determined to overcome her disability.

Every single day, Letty did many strenuous exercises that she found while investigating her illness in library books. The opinion of her doctors was that she would end up in a wheelchair. They said that there was nothing they could do to make her better. That leg was always going to be much weaker than the other.

My father wanted Letty to work in an office, but that's not what she wanted. She wanted to be a nurse, helping people. The nursing school in Amsterdam didn't want to take her because of her disability, so she went to the other end of the country and applied again, faking her disability. It worked. She did her training and did it well. Every day she continued her exercises on her leg. She began to play tennis and became really good at it. She skied and participated in all of the sporting events she could.

My amazing sister Letty became a better swimmer, bicycle rider, tennis player, and walker than me. The only thing I could beat her in was table tennis or badminton. She never let that polio get the best of her. Letty was very focused and determined, and overcame so many hurdles.

Today, Letty can still stand on her head and do the splits like a woman much younger. She's quite an inspiration and I'm so proud of her.

Written 2016

CHILDREN AND GRANDCHILDREN!

I am blessed with three children, nine grandchildren (one more is on the way), and three great-grandchildren.

Loretta has three boys—Casey, Garland, and Kenneth. Casey has baby William, and Garland has a boy, Zane, and a girl, Shayla.

Beatrix's daughter is Ariel, age twenty.

Guillermo's children are Sarah, Kateland, Bron, Koel, and Bela. They are expecting a new baby soon. Sarah has two children.

Guillermo's family lives in Temecula, so they don't come too often. I usually go to them.

When Bron was about three years old and Koel was almost two, I would sing to them *"Away in the manger, no crib for a bed."* I sang that song with the hand motions and they would look at me with those bright eyes in wonder. When Guillermo saw his little sons sing and do the motions with me, he sang with us too. We all sang it again and it felt so good.

Kenneth and Garland when they were young

I realized again that their parents didn't talk about Jesus or God. The songs the children hear are Rudolph the Red Nose Reindeer, Jingle bells, and other very nice songs, but no religious songs. It makes me sad. In my opinion every child should learn about God. I leave it alone and trust that God will take care of it.

One day when Guillermo was visiting, Bron, who was four at the time, asked his dad where his room used to be. Guillermo showed it to him and Bron wanted to lay down on the bed and said, "I want to feel my dad when he was a kid." Everybody always tells Bron how much he looks like his dad (he really does) and acts like him.

Then Koel, his younger brother said, "No, Oma, I'm like my dad. I'm smart. I will read you a story." I always have many books in the house and he picked one up from the children's books. Very seriously he read, "Brown bear, brown bear, WHAT DO YOU SEE? I see a cat looking at me. Brown bear, brown bear what do you see? I see a lion looking at me." And it goes on like that.

I was flabbergasted; not even three years old! He could read! Then I realized that he read it from memory. It was still amazing. He said, "I'm smart like my dad, and funny like my dad and I play ball with my dad. I just don't look like my dad." And, of course that is true.

My son Guillermo with daughters Kateland (l) and Sarah

Today Bron will go to second grade in September and Koel to kindergarten. And again, I realize how great it is to be a grandmother. I play, read, and talk to them but the responsibility lies with the parents.

Bron wants to learn and have friends but he doesn't like outside play. Koel loves to play outside, likes to learn sports.

Little Bela follows Koel in just about everything. And she too has that carefree attitude and Latin temper like Koel and their dad, when he was their age.

Hooray! They're coming and I love it.

Bron  *Koel*  *Bela*

HOW I ALMOST LOST MY GRANDDAUGHTER

One day nineteen years ago my son Guillermo called me and asked if Katie, his five-year-old daughter, was with me.

I said, "No, she's with Destiny, her mother." Guillermo and Destiny were divorced.

Guillermo said, "I called her and Ryan but nobody answers. Then I called Destiny's mother. She didn't know but thought they may be at her mom's place." Ryan was Destiny's new husband.

It was still early afternoon, so I said, "Don't worry, they must be on the beach or just out. Call later."

But he told me, "I have such a weird feeling that something is wrong. I will call Katie's great-grandma."

The great-grandmother lived in a community for senior citizens near Escondido. When he calls, she tells him that Katie, Destiny, and Ryan were out riding around on her golf cart.

Guillermo asks for someone to go and look for them because he tried to call but didn't get an answer. He still feels worried. Great-grandma realizes that they had been out for a while and said she would investigate.

In the meantime, Destiny's mother and my son decided to drive down there. At that time my son lived in Long Beach, quite far from the home of the great-grandma. When Destiny's mother arrived, there was quite a commotion

The golf cart had lost its brakes and drove into the ravine. Ryan told Destiny to jump and threw Katie out into the high trees. He went down and landed on the bottom. The ambulance and a helicopter were there.

Destiny landed with her head on a big stone and died very soon. She was pregnant and lost her baby as well. But Katie landed a ways down, all bloody but able to find a walking path.

She saw a truck and waved at the man and yelled, "My mom fell. She's up there!" He drove her up, saw her mother, and told Katie to stay in the car. They were taking Destiny away in the ambulance.

But then Katie screamed, "Ryan, Ryan is down there!" The

people with the helicopter were still there and investigated and indeed they found the golf cart upside down on the bottom. They got him out and flew him to the hospital. Katie went also.

Katie today (r) with her cousin Ariel

My son was instructed to go directly to the hospital where Katie was. She looked pretty bad, but nothing major was wrong.

Sadly, Destiny died and Ryan broke his back. He was one year in the hospital, but after that he got a lot better. Today he works and walks again. Katie had all scratches and scars, bleeding from her body, but by the Grace of God, she was fine and went home with her dad.

Today they still go to the spot on the day where the accident happened, once a year. Ryan, Katie, and my son, go to remember Destiny and how Katie was saved.

Katie lived with her dad from then on, coping with the memory and loss of her mother. She has finished high school, still studies, has a job, and is OK.

LAS VEGAS AND HAWAII

In 2008 I had just completed four very enjoyable days with Beatrix, Philip, and Ariel in Las Vegas. We walked around and admired the Vegas Strip. Ariel especially enjoyed the M&M Building, Coca Cola, and the white tigers. At the resort we enjoyed the swimming pools. Philip and I played in the casinos for a while in the evening. That was fun! We both won a little too. That was MORE fun!

Then I enjoyed Loretta's graduation. It was very impressive and of course I was very proud seeing her accept her Master's Degree in Spiritual Psychology. To celebrate, we took a trip to Hawaii.

When we arrived, we rented a car. Loretta and her friend Diana rented a jeep first. That was exciting but very, very unhandy. I could barely struggle into the front seat and neither of the girls could comfortably sit in the back seat. We exchanged it later in the afternoon and got a convertible Mustang. Very nice, but soon we realized how terribly windy it is in the back seat and how hard to get in and out. But we kept it anyway because it was fun and exciting to drive with the top down.

Our condo was on Kona in the WorldMark Resort and it was very comfy. I love to stay there. It has all the features one wants for a leisurely vacation. The first day we visited the city, beach, and stores. Lots of cute souvenirs and beautiful Hawaiian clothes. Loretta found a glorious dress. I found postcards galore. The girls went for a long walk while I stayed around the condo. We saw "Bosco," a musician who played several musical instruments and sang songs. Quite nice. I bought a video and a CD that we played so many times on the way back that we forgot it in the rented car. On purpose? Who knows? Most of the songs were about love and it coincided well with the spiritual degree Loretta and Diana had just earned.

Most of the beaches had rocks, but a few were beautiful with white sand. The water is so clear and pleasant—unreal! We found a semi-private beach and did some swimming and snorkeling. We saw many, many beautiful fish and Loretta came upon a giant turtle. Diana and I saw it too. It stayed around us for a short time. Really exciting for our first outing to the beach. Of course, we all three got a bad sunburn on our neck and shoulders from the snorkeling. After that day we always wore a T-shirt to prevent any more harm to our bodies.

The most exciting outing we took was swimming with the dolphins. The boat took us far into the ocean and when the crew saw a school of dolphins, they let us in the water to swim with them. The crew gave us equipment, snorkels, and fins, and I took a soft foam pad to help me float.

The first time I floated quietly and saw the dolphins swim under me. The smaller ones jumped up from the water. I was so comfortable and let myself float until I looked up and saw how far I was from the boat! I started to swim towards it a little panicky, but half way there I saw some white legs and Loretta was there to guide me.

When the dolphins left, we went back in the boat. The crew looked for more dolphins and let us out again. I went in twice and was exhausted. Loretta and Diana went in again. On the way back, they showed us part of the lava from the volcano going into the ocean. This is one of the reasons the island constantly changes.

Along the shore we did some snorkeling too. Here we saw even more beautiful fish. It was like swimming in a fantastic BIG aquarium full of wonderful, different species and sizes of fish. There were four crew members and eleven vacationers on the boat, so we were well protected. They also gave us lunch!

Our most interesting and fun boat trip was with Captain Zodiac for a rafting and snorkeling adventure. A young, handsome captain took us fourteen miles into the ocean on a raft about twelve feet long to Kealakekua Bay. We sat on top of the inflated tube sides of the raft, our feet under a rope for balance. There was a rope along the top of the tube that we held on to with our hands. Thank goodness the captain gave me a place close to him and I could hold on to the railing where the steering wheel was. We saw caves, lava tubes, amazing wildlife, more dolphins, and the most beautiful and plentiful fish while snorkeling. The captain told us many interesting stories about Hawaiian folklore and history, the Captain Cook monument, the different species of fish and coral, and more. Very interesting and entertaining. They also had snacks and juice.

Then we went on a small air plane. It was awesome. You could see the whole island and all the different aspects of it. Really fabulous. The only bad thing was that Loretta got air sick and threw up during almost the whole flight. That was very sad.

After that we took a break and just did some sightseeing and shopping. There was a Farmers Market with delicious fruit—*doerian* (sour sack), papaya, *pisang, radjak* (small very tasty bananas) *doekoe* (I think they call it here leechy), and of course mangos, etc. It was fun. We stopped by every day after that for an hour before we left for another adventure.

We also took a tour in our car all around the island. It was amazing how many different sceneries there were. Like the desert, rain forest, luscious greenery, and flowers. Twice we sighted an active volcano. Once we had to walk over volcanic rocks for about a half mile before we had a good look at it. Of course, Loretta and Diana took a "million" pictures, but so far, I have only seen them on their digital cameras. Very beautiful.

MEMORY LANE AND A RIVER TRIP

Last June I met with my three sisters, Nel, Letty, and Trix, in the Netherlands. The first day Trix, Let, and I relaxed at Letty's place in Castricum, Holland, which is a lovely small city close to the beach. We rode our bicycles to the beach in just twenty minutes. It was a nice ride through the dunes and woods. We could have taken the car, but then we would have had to pay for parking

The next day we went to see Nel. She's my second oldest sister at the ripe age of eighty-seven. She lives in a home for elderly people. I had not seen it yet and I was pleasantly surprised by how nice it was. She had her own apartment, but the staff had a key to it and checked on her twice a day, or whenever she called them. She could eat at home or go down to the dining room. There were chairs and tables and nice sofas to sit down and have coffee. Nel's son Walter comes to see her almost every day. He often cooks and makes her coffee or tea and gets her some things from the store. If she wants to go out, he helps her.

After we met and said our hellos, we played bridge. This is our family game. At eighty-seven, Nel still played a good game. We enjoyed it a lot. We spoke about "old times" and how we used to play at home, and in the camp, and how I had to often play because Claar didn't want to. I played back then with my mother, Fransje, and Nel. This game helped us through many difficult times, during and after the camp. It's remarkable that we, the four youngest of the children (three to seven years old at the time), played this complicated game too. At least we tried. We did take it seriously. It helped us pretend to be in another world, concentrating on nothing but the game.

After playing for over three hours, Letty and I left for Doorn where her daughter Petra lives. It was the birthday of Zoe, Petra's daughter. So, we visited them and enjoyed the kids party. Then we went to a Thai, Chinese, and Indonesian restaurant. Jeroen, Petra's husband, picked up Nel and Trix to meet us at the restaurant.

The food was delicious, buffet style. Then of course, they came with a birthday cake for Zoe. What a joy that was! Let and I went back with Petra and spent the night. Jeroen drove Trix and Nel back to Nel's place. The next day Let and I rode to Nel's home where we played bridge again, also with Nel's son, Walter.

Together we went to the home of Letty's son Gert. He's self-employed, so he was home making a delicious Indonesian meal. He loves to cook, he is so good at it! His wife works, so she likes it too! We spent the day with Gert and by ten in the evening he took us to Arnhem where we boarded the cruise ship, which took us on the Rijn and Mosselle rivers—from the Netherlands through Belgium and Germany.

Trixie, Letty, and I had a cabin for three. When we arrived, they served us some wine and snacks. The next morning all the other passengers came on board. There were ninety-five passengers altogether. I never was on a river cruise or on such a small ship. I was so pleasantly surprised at how nice it was. They were all Dutch, so we could speak our own language. Everybody was so happy, friendly, and ready to have a good time.

There was always something to do. We played card games or checkers in the lounge. There was always coffee or wine and a snack. Up on deck was also very nice. They had plenty of beach chairs with cushions. Every morning we did thirty minutes of exercises, which was fun. Of course, the scenery was gorgeous, with so much luscious green landscape and flowers, quaint castles, beautiful small houses, wind mills, and many wineries growing up into the hills.

Breakfast, lunch, and dinner were served in the dining room and most of the time it was real Dutch food. Delicious! I tasted all the delicious different kinds of bread, cheese, vegetables, and deserts, and of course, always fruit. They had a snack in the afternoon with good wine or coffee.

For entertainment, we either played games, went to one of the small cities, or visited some castles. We had wine tasting, a sip of five different wines, and we got one bottle free! Of course, we also bought a few to share with our family when we went back.

In the evening they always had a game, puzzle, music, or some type of show. Trixie and I loved it especially because they sang all the old Dutch songs. We danced, did the polonaise and other dances. The last evening, they had a musician/singer. He was fun and good, playing all the old Dutch songs and more. He played several instruments and was quite a comedian. All those who could, danced and sang along. Letty and Trix were always ready to join in with me. It was very pleasant and fun, it made me think of all the good times I had during the eight years I lived in Holland.

I'm so glad I made the trip, it really helped me bond with the people I come from. My sister Trixie really wanted to make this river cruise through Holland and Germany. She had a mighty struggle with cancer recently. She's a bit better now! Who knows, the trip might have given her a new jump into life!

MY GRANDSON'S WEDDING

My grandson Garland met Theresa in college in Oceanside. They both took a dance class—ballroom dancing. Soon they became good dancing partners and fell in love. After a year or so they broke up. Garland felt that he wasn't ready to work full time, go to college, and become a husband as well.

They both felt so miserable and couldn't stay away from each other. So, he bought her a promise ring and a year later, in 2013, they were ready to marry.

The ceremony was outside at the Anaheim Hills Country Club. Right on top of the hill. The view was so gorgeous. She had a princess dress on, he a tux. The setting sun made the few clouds glow softly orange and gold. It was as if the Lord gave His blessing and all the angels were there in the sky playing and dancing with joy. The bridal pair looked so happy and sincere, ready to take on all their challenges from now on with a loving partner.

Garland and Theresa

MY FAVORITE BIRTHDAY

In 2015 my lovely daughter Loretta asked me, "What would you like to do on your eightieth birthday?"

I said, "I just want a party in my house with family and some friends."

Well, I sure got a party! She and my son and his family helped to decorate everything beautifully, hired someone to play my favorite music, and invited my friends from my bridge club, writing class, and other friends and neighbors. Oh, my gosh, there were so many people to celebrate with me. I talked and joked with many. Some I hadn't seen for quite a while. We played some games, had some drinks and snacks. There was lots of room in front as well as in the back yard.

Around six o'clock a delicious Indonesian dinner was served. There were many dishes. There was plenty for everybody and something that each person would like. Indonesian food is somewhat like Thai food. Bron and Koel, my grandsons, were helping to serve many ladies who wanted punch. Bela, my three-year-old granddaughter, danced so cute and was very friendly to all my guests. We all danced a little. The real dancers danced a lot. Most of us did the polonaise, including little Bela.

We all had so much fun. Loretta had a beautiful big cake with a picture of a beautiful lady on it! Me!! It was delicious and enough for everybody. I felt so special and appreciated by all. We even had a place we could make pictures with big hats, or other decorations. What fun we had! Thank you all. It was the best party ever!

A WONDERFUL REUNION

July 22, 2016, on my birthday, I sat on the plane with nine family members to start our trip to the reunion in Belgium. We arrived at Schiphol, Holland, the next day, drove to the Castle (Chateau De Blier) in Erezee, Belgium. It was a feast to be with so many of our family. Our younger family members had so much fun, talking for hours together, playing games to no end.

My sister Letty and I were the oldest ones. All my other siblings are gone or too elderly or sick to travel. It was great to see everybody having so much camaraderie and fun. Many folks brought their children. Some I met for the first time. The kids all got along and were so good together! It is amazing to have family living in three countries, so far from each other, still finding time every five years to travel, be together. We also find that we have many of the same likes and habits!

Our surroundings in Erezee, Belgium, were beautiful, with lush green grass, trees, flowers, small houses, and old buildings from the late 1800s. There were many friendly little villages, lots of beautiful parks and small courts. There were glorious plants and flowers on almost every crossing or in front of big, modern buildings. There was so much water from the sky, in the ground, small streams, ponds, on our heads, and on the grass, everywhere!!

We loved the quaint small eateries with delicious specialties—thin pancakes with fresh fruit and whipped cream, cheese and fruit, meats and spices, every kind you can think of. I remember when I was in Miami, Florida, we found pizza with toppings of whatever you can think of too, even with chocolate! Great!

And everywhere there was Belgium beer! Delicious! I'm not a beer drinker, but that beer was outstanding!

We visited many attractions, like small beautiful gardens and museums of all kinds. We also explored the caves discovered there. One had the longest and deepest waterway below the ground. I couldn't walk through the cave because the ground went up and down and there were stairs in places. So, I took the boat.

Many times, I had to lay flat down so that we could go under the rocks. The captain laid flat too, pulling the boat further on. At one stop, we picked up all the tired people and floated down on a bigger stream. It was beautiful, colorful, and eerie too. Things sounded strange so far under the ground.

Then people walked again on those small, slippery stairs. I went back with that boat and continued through those low and narrow waterways. This time the captain used a stick to push us along. It was very interesting, but I won't do it again!

On the last two days my nephew Gert had arranged a special gathering, but his new baby came early. He had to turn over responsibility for the gathering to his daughter, son, and a cook. All three were under twenty years old, and they did a good job. Gert brought his wife Natasha and their two-week old baby, Carmen, to meet the whole gang. Carmen is the newest member of our family, the youngest one to ever attend our fantastic family reunions!

(l-r) Trixie, Me, and Letty

When I came home, I got a very nice birthday card from my friends at my writing class. All was well with me and all the animals, but not at home! There was no television, no telephone, no internet, my suitcase lost, and my gate broken! So, all those good and well wishes were just what I needed. Your nice wishes and memories of our class made me feel so good. You all are just "the bomb," as my daughter would say.

OUR SOUTH AMERICAN RELATIVES

Family gatherings I enjoy very much. One of the last ones included visitors from Colombia, South America. My son's father came over for a month, with his wife Martha, his daughter Dominique, and his sister Laura. My son lives in Wildomar, California, so they spent half of the time with him or me. Sometimes all together.

We had fun together, went to the beach, played tennis (not me), saw a movie, and played games together. We often played Scrabble and several card games—rummy (with "May I"), charades, and the newest one, "Cards Against Humanity." They visited with their friends and close family here a few times. I didn't join them. I needed a break!

I stayed close with my ex's family ever since the divorce. He remarried, I did not. Their daughter Dominique is now sixteen years old and a typical teen-ager with "holes" in her pants, leggings, nose rings, and more. She is my son Guillermo's half-sister, and so she is an aunt to Katie, even though the two are close in age. Dominique speaks excellent English. I treated Dominique and my granddaughters Katie and Ariel to a day at Knotts Berry Farm together. They could bond, have lots of fun.

We went five days to Indio, to a WorldMark resort, with all of us—nine Acostas and me! It was so much fun. Not only are there several swimming pools, but also there is a pool where the current goes around and around. We loved that. Sat in big, round plastic floats.

We also played in the Sports Room—ping-pong, all kinds of machines, shuffle board, and more. We even saw a movie! Had an ice cream social. It all was so much fun. All the kids and adults could swim, including Bela, who just turned three years. But her mother insisted that she wear a swim-vest. We all are water lovers. It was blazing hot, so that was very important. Our rooms were air conditioned and comfy.

I stayed home when they were at my son Guillermo's place. He took them to some wineries in Temecula, the beaches, lunch and more. They even, in spite of the hot weather, played tennis several times. They all had a great time. We did too.

Laura is still here. She had a pass for six months and wanted to explore California. She's staying with my son and Karen, helping with the three kids and learning English. She's teaching the kids Spanish. Bela is able to pick up a lot and so is Koel, but Bron isn't all that interested. He is eight years old. It's really true that a younger child can learn a new language faster. I'm happy, and hope they will keep it up.

Katie, my son's older daughter, speaks good Spanish and my son speaks the language fairly well. I think that everybody in California should speak English and Spanish. Other countries can teach their children another language, so why not the United States? If we all speak two languages, especially in California, then the Spanish-speaking people who come here will want to learn English fast. Otherwise they will never get a decent job. But that's just my idea.

On July 4th, our big celebration of freedom, we had a "block" party. All the neighbors in our block participated. It was fabulous. Not only because of the fireworks, but because all of my family was here. My two daughters and my son with his whole gang. He had nice fireworks for the kids. Lots of sparkles, not those very loud ones that sound like shots. Three of my direct neighbors had the same but others had those loud ones. All went well, it was fun. Even our dogs and cats weren't that scared until much later at night. At that time, we were all in the house.

MOTHER'S DAY 2018

Are they coming? I'm not sure who and when, we'll see. I had a splintered toe some four weeks ago and was in a cast twice, and then a boot. I also had an operation on my poor nose to remove a cancer. It took over two hours to do. Even with all of this, I went in my car and did some shopping for the party!

I had made their most favorite peanut butter sauce (Indonesian style) the night before. I went to the store where I bought ready-to-eat barbecued chicken and many vegetables, some to eat raw and some to steam, all delicious with the sauce I made. That was all I could do at this time of my life.

I washed and cleaned the vegetables, got my paper plates out and more. This is unusual for me because I don't like to eat from paper or plastic, but considering my condition, I had no choice.

Loretta had taken me out for a delicious dinner the night before with her son's family, which was sooo much fun. She had made a fantastic cake. The leftovers she would take to my party. So, I was ready!! At three o'clock nobody was there yet, but I was expecting that, so I had time to take a little nap in my favorite chair before they came.

By four o'clock Beatrix called and said she Ariel were on their way. Soon after, Loretta said the same. By five o'clock my son and his family were present too. Hooray, my three children were there! What a joy! They all love each other, but are so different. They don't really do things together, other than most family-related outings. They're all loud, joking and teasing each other. My son's three younger children are adorable. So, the gang is here!!

First, I had to show them my flowers. Maybe they are not too enthusiastic about them, but I am. I appreciated their interest. I have mostly cactuses, so many in bloom. Unbelievably beautiful. Mostly big white flowers, some red or pink (the small ones), also some in my back yard, absolutely red and gorgeous!

My peach tree, that I planted last year, was full of fruit! This is rare, because the fruit on my other trees are often eaten by birds before I can pick any.

This time I have Peanut, my black cat that I got from my friend Kay from the writing class. Her cat had five kittens! Loretta took one and she's with me!! She's a real joy, so playful with me, skittish to most others, but she's my joy and sweetheart. Birthday, my other cat, originally came from Loretta. She's sweet, mostly in the house.

Peanut however is outside a lot. She chases everything—small birds, which I don't like but I accept because she's a cat! Sometimes I see her racing up the tree after squirrels, which is so funny and interesting to follow. A squirrel would go from the top of the tree over the cable line to the shack (which is below) and wait on the cable, daring Peanut. Peanut would come to the top of the tree and sit where the cable is, daring the squirrel to come closer to play in "her" tree. They play "cat and mouse."

I have several bird feeders, but lately I don't fill them because Peanut chases the birds and has caught some. That breaks my heart. But how can I be angry with her? She's a cat and that's what cats do.

I'm very proud of her when she scares the gophers away. I had a real bad time with them before she came, but no more!! She also caught some mice, so I have none of those pests anymore. Unfortunately, the neighbors still have gophers. Mice, I don't know.

I also have two dogs. Mine is a very small Yorkie terrier, Honey. Loretta has the same type of dog too, Lucas. I watch Lucas every day while Loretta works, or Lucas needs to be watched. I love him and he gets along fine with Honey, although they don't play together. Lucas is one year younger than Honey. I rescued Honey when she was almost five years old. She was in real bad shape. The vet said she would not make it more than about five months.

But I fell in love with her, took her in, gave her the best of care. Well, she turned out to be a beauty. So sweet and lovable. Coming October, she'll be fifteen years old. Unfortunately, she's blind now, can't hear, and lost all her teeth two years ago. She also can't walk good because of her damaged paws.

She does eat well and knows me. I guess she can still smell. She wants to be with me all the time. Never complains or whines.

Me and Honey

    She often gets "lost" in the house and/or outside between the plants and all. But she gives her little "bark" and I follow the sound and find her. You can't believe the places she gets stuck in. She's so small, only two pounds now. Lucas is still four pounds.

    To come back to my "Happy Mother's Day" visitors.

    They were all here. We made pictures, sang songs and had lots of fun, joking about "old times." My son's dad was with us. He moved back to Colombia after he retired. We all love each other and accept each other. I have always stayed friends with him. He's my son's dad! That's what I always wanted to teach my children, to love and accept each other as we are, no matter what we do or believe in. We are family. We had a great and lovely time together.

MOMENTS

WHAT MAKES ME HAPPY

I am almost eighty-three years old. I love to see, talk to, and be with my family. I love to get up with a lot of sunshine, have my coffee early in the morning with my lovely little Honey and Lucas, my miniature Yorkie's, and two cats, Birthday and Peanut. They all greet me with love and adoration. I love them all. It also makes me happy to see all or even a few of my flowers greeting me. They're so pretty and full of life. I guess I like the mornings the best.

I also like to play bridge with my friends, have lunch and be with them, go to my writing class, be among a bunch of nice people and work on my memoirs I like to write and finish before it's too late!

I love to see my daughter Loretta coming home from work. She brings her little Yorkie Lucas before she goes to work and picks him up after work. We often watch a program on television, have dinner, and just talk some. She often takes me out to eat in various restaurants. It really makes me happy if I can ride with her to family events and other parties or outings. She lives the closest to me, she's always kind, but doesn't always agrees with me which is OK, too.

I also love to be with my son's family, I love his children and they love me too. I'm also happy when I see Beatrix, my other daughter. She helps me with my computer. I really appreciate that, she's patient and doesn't get frustrated with me! And, of course I love to be with all my other family.

I love to go places, see my faraway family. Explore their surroundings. Go on cruises, even though I feel that I'm getting too old for that now. I've been on many cruises and travels to other countries. I would still go with a loving family member, or, if I had an older friend or friends, but it has to be on a slower pace.

Written 2018

MY SPECIAL TALENTS

I think that I have many talents. I play sports—tennis, badminton, table tennis, bowling, volleyball, swimming, bicycling, sailing, fishing, golf, and more! I also dance, play bridge and many other card games. Board games, too. I come from a big family and we always played games, later a lot of sports and competitions.

My mother taught me to sew and I became a fairly good seamstress. I used that talent a lot when I first came to the USA. Made my little girls many a costume. For my son I made an "ET, go home" costume from the movie. It took seven yards of material. The face was specially embroidered. My children won many a prize with these costumes.

I had to make my oldest daughter's pants or dresses longer. She was way too tall for the sizes here. I also made many Halloween costumes to sell. It was fun and I made extra money with it. I found jobs almost immediately in all the countries where I have lived. Here in the USA I found the best job. For six years I sold Sovereign House Crystal. Later it changed to Princess House Crystal. I did really well, sold a lot, had many parties, had several ladies who worked for me.

It was so fun! I won several prizes like a trip to London, Majorca, the Caribbean, and to a sailboat adventure, followed with a Boston crab feast in the evening. That was great. There were only five salespersons, besides the captain, the Boss, and three young men who helped the captain and served us food and drinks. Those were the best few days I ever had, and that was the best job I ever had. I could do much work at home and make really good money.

MY POSITIVE INFLUENCES AS A CHILD

I was born in Padang, Indonesia. I had already three sisters and two brothers. All I can remember is that I idolized my mother, but she didn't have much time for me. I was too often with my oldest sister Francisca or with the *baboe* (our nanny). My brother Jan, born thirteen months earlier, was often sick and got much attention.

Growing up I remember that my father left early in the morning and said, "Good morning," and kissed us all. Then he left for work. We saw him mostly just before dinner time. I remember vaguely that he usually had a drink with Mother and then we ate and we all had a chance to share something. When it was my turn, I always had something, a bug or flower, or just some lines on a paper. It was fun because everybody gave me attention then.

My father was the one who had to punish us if we did something wrong or bad. He never, ever spanked anyone of us, but we got a "talk" or just an angry look. I was only six years when we were put in a concentration camp because the Japanese army had come to take Indonesia. They took our dad away. I really don't remember much from before, only good things. Unfortunately, I remember well from that time on.

In the beginning of our time in prison camp my mother was always optimistic and dealt with each ordeal as best she could. But Fransje, my oldest sister, took over more and more responsibility. Fransje taught us to write letters and numbers. Mother read us books or told us stories. What I remember most was the soft singing to praise God.

I was always with my two younger sisters and my brother Jan. In the beginning we played on the street but pretty soon we stopped. No challenge or energy. My sister Francisca made us remember what she taught us and she told us that someday, when we got out of the camp, we would eat what we wanted and wash ourselves with lots and lots of water, etc. I guess she influenced us the most.

My mother mostly took things as they came and apologized for the life we had now. But even at seven or eight years old, I knew that it was wrong. That it wasn't right that those soldiers could boss us around and be mean. Maybe that is why I was told to never say anything and absolutely not look any of them in the eye. I had blue eyes. The others had my father's brown eyes, Fransje had gray ones. The soldiers had hit Fransje in the beginning because she had light eyes, and I hated them all. We had a good idea of what they would do to me if they saw my blue ones.

It was Fransje who told me that it was OK when I got my "period." I was only eleven years old. My sister Claar had gotten hers when she was seventeen and I heard them talk about it as if it wasn't good. It was Fransje who talked to me about that and sex.

Later on, when I was fourteen, I talked to mother and found out that she wasn't too informed about that. My parents were strict Catholics and that was not discussed. It was then that I became very close to my mother. She became my friend too. I loved and understood many things about her life and my father's life.

They were both honest and simple in their belief in love for each other, their children, and in Christianity. My mother has been not only my mother, but also my friend from then on until she died. I still miss her terribly.

MORE LIKE MOTHER OR DAD?

When I was young, I always looked more like my father, except for my blue eyes. He was very handsome, I had a very even face, small nose, ears, and lips, and heavy eyebrows. My hair was blond, but wavy. I was well proportioned, good looking. As it turned out, I was also very strong, responsible, and had a soft and sensual way of looking at life. Also tough with myself and tight with my money. Easily hurt or offended by other people. Just like my dad.

My mother was very sweet and pretty too, but in a different way. She had a big nose, brown hair, blue eyes, and thicker lips. She was a happier person, free with her money, and very sweet for her children. Always saw the best in people and very helpful and encouraging to us. Everybody liked her and admired her for her kindness and helpfulness. I adored my mother. But I was not so "adorable and lucky" as she was.

Later in life I got to know my dad and saw my likeness in him. I could talk to him, but usually in a serious way, or about interesting stories in his life away from us. And about his opinion about the world around us. He was often helpful and encouraging. He always knew when I was down or something was bothering me. I could tell him if something happened to me that I would never tell my mother.

Pa hardly ever talked about the bad things that happened to him, but he did so sporadically with me, especially when we were in Holland and my mother went to Canada for six months.

My mother's mother was still alive, but she was in a rest home. Pa came almost every day to take Oma out to the garden for a while and I came on Saturdays and Sundays for a couple of hours. Oma died and my mother came back immediately. She knew that her mother didn't suffer or miss her, because Oma thought that I was her daughter and my dad was very kind to her. My mother was the sunshine of his life and all our lives. I often wished that I could be more trusting and carefree like my mother.

WHEN I AM HARD ON MYSELF

I don't really know why or what it is. I'm always sorry that I didn't provided any of my children with a good father. I tried to be a super good mother, but I know that I'm not really. But I tried!

Why does one think that I love or care more about one child or the other? I love my three children equally. They're so different. I tried to show them that I do love and appreciate them equally. I think that each one is very special, smart, and lovely in their own way. I consider myself very lucky to have them.

My life isn't perfect, I think that's not supposed to be so. We make the best of it, be happy, live an honest life, and appreciate what we have. Be able to accept whatever is in store for us, be able to accept that. And when it's time to leave this world, I hope to find all my loved ones again.

CONCERTS!

One of the first concerts I attended was when I was fifteen years old and living with my parents in Amsterdam. I had a really nice girlfriend, Loes. We often went out on our bicycles all over Amsterdam. We both already had boyfriends. They were in the service.

Well, Louie Armstrong was coming to the concert hall of Amsterdam. They usually only presented classical music or operas in that building. One gets dressed real nice and never makes noise once the event begins.

Louie came and his concert was very different. It was very loud. His band was great and he sang beautifully. We loved it and, yes, we all made a lot of noise, stood on chairs, were very excited and wild. I was already hooked on theater and concerts. Now even more.

When I was living in Montreal, I had a year ticket that gave me ten plays or concerts. I saw one with Liberace. He played the piano so wonderfully and his outfits were great. It was so different. I could have sat there all night, forever listening to him.

Even here in Los Angeles, some concerts stand out for me. I can remember the *Hunchback of the Notre Dame*, and Julie Andrews in the *Sound of Music*. She plays a nanny. She and the seven children leave their homeland because of the Nazis. She sings the Edelweiss song, Snow White, and more.

I even saw one concert with my teen-aged son Guillermo, *Regge Music*. Here in California. It was sure interesting. The performer even came over to shake my son's hand! Oh, I loved and enjoyed them all. Too bad I had to quit these outings due to no time and no money. This changed my pleasures to children's outings, camping, and more. The world is just so expensive now!

RESENTMENTS

The first time I experienced resentment, I was about seven years old. We, (the white Dutch people) were in a concentration camp under the Japanese regime during World War II in Indonesia.

My mother and I were the only ones in our family of ten who had blue eyes. During a squabble with a Japanese soldier over something we were not supposed to do, he looked at me, and I made eye contact! How could I? I was instructed never to show my eyes to Japanese soldiers. For many years I felt resentment about this. Later I realized that it wasn't personal, it was just hating towards anyone with blue eyes.

The second time I felt resentment was towards my husband. After nine years of marriage, and six years more of trying to get pregnant and finally consulting a doctor, Ger and I had a daughter.

After a few weeks he told me that he never even wanted children. After six months he left me with the baby and all the bills. What a selfish coward! Now I'm glad we divorced because I never would have been happy with him anyway, even though the resentment is still there, and sometimes it still hurts. I just left Canada and made a new life for us here in the United States.

The third time I felt resentment was when I was forty-seven years old. I started a new profession after I lost my previous business because I was sick for three months.

I studied for fourteen months, got my diploma, did my last rotation of internship in Beverly Hospital, got my license, and they asked me to accept a position with them. I did and for twelve years it was great. I often worked overtime, and on my days off. In January, two of the thirty-two employees in our department got a "merit" raise. I was one of them.

Soon after, I had some personal problems and couldn't do all that overtime anymore. I still did my work well, never missed a day. When I was fifty-nine, I found out that they were checking me constantly. Sure enough, they asked me to take a leave of absence because my work was all of a sudden "not up to par." I was shocked and said NO. Then they threatened to lay me off.

I knew that they had to cut back about ten percent of our

personnel, but why me? Because I was the oldest? White? That I hardly ever was sick and was now taking the days off instead? I made some errors but everybody makes them. They weren't bad. I had resentment toward them and the hospital. So, I quit.

Thanks to my children I got over it. I'm happy now and know that it wasn't my fault. I also know that I could have fought it in court successfully. I also knew that it would have ruined me emotionally. I choose to quit and let it go.

These are the three resentments I had to cope with during my life. I hope by writing this, I help someone who's in a similar situation and tell them not to let it ruin them.

FEELING ALONE

This is a difficult question. I've really never been all alone. My mother and dad were there and my many siblings. Later when I met my first husband, Gerrit, he was always there. And already, at a very young age, I always knew that I had an angel from above watching over me.

I think the first time I felt totally alone was when Ger and I went out with another couple. Ger took off with the wife and let me stay home with the husband. I knew Ger did it on purpose. The husband tried to make love to me, but I could not do it. I left, walked on the railroad tracks, wanting to die. At six in the morning, I turned around and went home. Ger was home, making coffee—never saying anything. He had a sly smile on his lips. I said, "You didn't win, I didn't do it."

The second time I felt totally alone was when my oldest daughter Loretta played clarinet and won an award. I was so proud, but I had no one to share it with. My children Beatrix and Guillermo were there, but they were still so young and didn't understand my happiness. A similar thing happened some years later when my son won a speech contest over seven schools. He gave a speech in the church, full of people. But I sat alone in that church—his dad didn't show up, he didn't care.

In spite of that, I consider myself lucky to have had parents who taught me to believe in God and that you're really never alone then. I think that's why I'm mostly happy and content with my life, although I always wanted to have a soul mate to share it with but was never able to find one. Now I have three wonderful children, many grandchildren and great grandchildren. My wish was always that my children would find a soul mate, and I pray for this every day.

I SEE YOU, BUT I DON'T KNOW YOU

Yes, there are some people I have seen all the time for the last thirty years and yet I don't know them. One such a person is my lawn man. I always come out, pay him, ask how he is, exchange some news, or comment about the weather. Sometimes we talk about my yard and my plant hobby.

I know his name, but not where he lives or how many kids he has. I know one son for sure because he helps him sometimes. I like him, but I'm not a person to ask personal questions. I guess he's the same. We smile at each other, exchange some comments and go on our way.

I have the same relationship with my mailman. I do like him. He has always something nice to say or he tells me a short story of what he saw or read. Then we each go our merry ways.

I have the same with many of my friends in my writing class or bridge clubs. There are just a few who tell me something personal, then I tell them mine. That's the first step to getting close and forming a relationship. Often it stops there.

I always have had and still have very few friends who I really know or who know me. I always wondered why, maybe because I'm so close with my family. At my more advanced age now, I think it's because I'm different than most people. Until I came to Norwalk (of all places), I was never more than, at the most, three years in the same place. That is spread out over four countries. I feel neither Indo-Dutch, Netherlander, Canadian, nor USA citizen. I can claim them all, but I feel that I really belong nowhere. So that's why I think I have few real friends. The ones I have I really cherish.

MY LIVELY CHILD

Beatrix turned out to be the liveliest child I ever came across. When she was barely six months she managed to climb out of her crib and fell on her head! At nine months, she walked like a pro and played games with us.

Once when she was two years old, we played Hide and Seek, and we couldn't find her anywhere! We alerted the neighbors and finally called the police. Everyone searched for her all over the street. Finally, after almost giving up, there she was! She had fallen asleep under the clothes in the hamper while hiding. She just came walking out like nothing happened. We were so relieved to see her, and so frustrated with her at the same time.

Beatrix learned to swim very quickly when she was only a year old. I took her to Mommy and Me swimming lessons. Mostly she swam under the water. Often, I was ready to dive in after her because she was under for so long, and then she would pop up out of the water with a big grin on her face! She scared us all plenty of times!

In 1969 I drove to California with Loretta, age six, Beatrix, age three, my mom, and a girlfriend of mine. Motel 6 was our place to stay, if they had a swimming pool. The first time we stopped at one, Beatrix jumped in the pool, clothes and all. I was in the office and I heard a BIG splash when my mom jumped in the pool after Bea! Then I had to jump in to save them both. What a commotion!! All three of us were fully clothed, too!

Once we went to the big Olympic-sized pool at Bell High School when Beatrix was about four years old, and they would not let her swim in the deep end because she was too small. In order to prove that she could swim, they made her swim up and back from one end of the pool to the other. She did it just fine! Once she was allowed in the deep end, we could all swim together.

I was watching Loretta show me her newest lifeguard training moves, and all of a sudden, we heard screaming. A lady was yelling, "OH MY GOD! Look at the baby!" I looked up and there was Bea, at the top of the high diving board ready to jump off. The life guards sprang into action, and raced up the stairs to get her. Just before they reached her, she laughed and jumped into the water. It looked so far down, with her little body flying through the air like that! She hit the water and disappeared. Everyone was shocked, and all of the staff were running around, jumping in the water, and very upset. Then, POOF, there was her head, popping up out of the water with a big laugh. We got kicked out of the pool that day, which was not fair, since she was fine and could swim just great!

A year after we arrived in California, we went to a park to play with our children. All of a sudden, where is Beatrix!? We found her in a light pole high up! She could not come down! We had to call the fire truck to help us out. Oh yes, everybody thought it was funny, but not me!

I can go on for many stories to come, but I will rest after this last story. One day we were at the beach and all of a sudden, she was gone. We again looked everywhere, and with the help of the life guard, we finally found her about a mile away, hiding in a deep hole with her head down. She just looked up at us with that scary look on her face and said, "I knew you would find me!" She really liked to scare us to death! She has not changed much.

Beatrix is now a Registered nurse and has worked in hospitals since her seventeenth birthday. Even now she still tells jokes, usually about gas, poo, or blood—you get the idea. This upsets some people but makes others laugh too. Ah well, that's my Beatrix!

FUNNY FAMILY FOLKS

My late brother Piet always made us laugh with things he said, or did, or with appropriate jokes. My sister Nel would often say or do something totally out of context that had nothing to do with what we were saying or doing. Her husband would slap his knee and say, "Ah that's our Nel," and laugh.

My little granddaughter Bela is funny. Sometimes she walks or hops like an animal (she's almost three now) or, just out of the blue, she dances and twirls around. She's such a comic and has so much fun that you have to laugh about it. When she laughs, you have to laugh also.

Then you have my sister Claar. She was funny in a different way. On a vacation in Hawaii we all went to a place where they make and sell jewelry. We all bought something, but not Claar! Later on she went back and bought something anyway. When we would go out to eat, she would claim not to be hungry, but later she would take a bite from us all, stating that she just wanted a taste. That way she never had to pay for food.

Then one night, we were sleeping in three connected rooms. She had a single bed in the room with my brother Piet and his wife. Well, in the middle of the night she let a very loud fart, like a cannon ball! Piet jumped up from his bed, and we, in the other rooms yelled, "What's happening!?" It was so loud, and Claar never woke up!

Even I made my family laugh. When we came to Holland right after the war, there were only black and white movies. But there was a theater that showed news or short documentary movies, which my mother thought were appropriate for us. I was then nine years old and never in a theater before. The documentary film was *How to Enjoy Life*. But there were no more tickets and I started to scream and cry, "I want to see how to enjoy my life!" Everybody looked at me and burst out laughing.

I could go on, but this is enough! LOL.

RESCUED AGAIN

The second time I was rescued from the water I was much older, swimming in the ocean. This time in Laguna Beach, California. I was with my son and his family but they weren't in the water. There were a few people in the water, I swam close to them.

And sure, enough a big wave came and I tumbled down, not able to come up fast. I felt the next one coming. I frantically waved at my son, but he waved back, not noticing that I was in trouble. I was much older then and not so strong anymore, so I panicked.

And what do you know! A strong young man was near me. He tried to go back too and I motioned to him and yelled if I could hold on to him. He came closer and just before I started to lose my legs, I got a hold of him. He helped me back. I thanked him profusely. My son and others didn't notice anything. I said nothing to anyone. But as of today, I only go as far as my knees in the water—unless I'm in a swimming pool!!

DO I BELIEVE IN GOD?

Oh, this is a deep question! I believe that whatever happens to us has a reason. I had a very rough life in my younger years. Later, from age eleven to about thirty years old, I had a good time. My teenage years were fun and ambitious. I had a good relationship with my family. I got married, went to Montreal, and even that was good for about eight years. I did have my wish—my baby girl was healthy and well. Later I had my second baby girl.

Then everything else went wrong. My father died, my husband disappeared, and my mother went back to Holland. Also, Montreal and the entire province of Quebec changed to a predominately French-speaking province. Many of the English companies moved to Ontario. The firm I worked for moved also. I sold my beautiful house with all the furniture, the car, and more, and stayed home looking after my girls for three years.

By then I could not find a good job anymore. My mother knew how disappointed and scared I was for the future. She said, "Why don't you take my car and drive to California? I come with you, also your girlfriend, and of course your lovely little girls." I did what she suggested.

I had a very hard time in California once my mother and friend went back to Canada. I got a job, but mostly everything else didn't go so well.

If I had not gone through such hard years as a child, I would not have survived all the obstacles I had. So, does that mean I believe in a higher power? God? Maybe.

I do believe strongly in my guardian angel. She was there in 1981 when I drove from California to Montreal for a visit. It was 3500 miles one-way and a six-week trip. I was with my two girls, my son, and Casey my grandson.

I never had a flat tire or broke down. Sometimes my family drove me crazy during the drive, but we made it, had a lot of fun too. On the way, we stopped at the Grand Canyon. We took some donkeys and rode, very slowly, step by step, down to the first stop. Then we walked back!! Oh, that was so hard. But we made it without big problems.

After that I drove home. We went over a bridge and found out that I went the wrong way, I tried to turn around, until Loretta yelled, "Mom, Mom, I don't see any street anymore!" She was in the back seat looking backwards.

I stopped immediately and found out that my back wheels were about two inches from the cliff. You think that I don't believe in my guardian angel? You bet I do. Is that a higher power? Who knows?

Another time I was driving to St. Francis Hospital to work. It was very cloudy and misty. I could hardly see a few feet ahead of the car. I had my high beams on and drove on Imperial Hwy. under the bridge on the wrong side of the road!

Oh, my goodness, was I scared! But again, my guardian angel made sure no other car came from the other side! You see I really believe in my guardian angel. Is she sent by a higher power?

Who knows, I'm just glad that I have her!

HEROES

As a small child, my hero was my father. He was so handsome and everybody loved him. What he said was law. And he gave us all a little time even though he was often away or very busy. Pa also gave us all a different name. My name was *ticoes*, that means small mouse in Malay, because I was skinny and had a small pointy face, I guess. It was used as an endearment.

When I got older, I had no heroes. Besides my family there wasn't anyone who I admired or wanted to be like. Most adults were disappointing. When the movies came out, I liked Doris Day, Fred Astaire and others.

When I was in Canada, I worked for the Sun Life Insurance Company. I had a very good boss. His name was Mr. Trenouph. He was kind, smart, fair, and played good bridge. I played bridge once a week in the evening in the company's bridge club. I played with my mother, later with Ger, my husband. My boss asked me to keep score and the next day he would come and sit on my desk and discus the bridge game. I felt so special.

When I came out of the camp, I had great respect for the soldiers, saw them as heroes. They defeated the enemy. No matter who or what they were or looked like—Gurkhas, English, Dutch, American—when I saw them, I admired them so much. I still do. Not so much the person himself, but what they stand for. They are truly HEROES.

ADVICE ON RAISING CHILDREN

Through my more than eighty years of living and raising my children and helping to raise my grand-children, I come to this advice:

Try to stay home or stay as many hours a day with your children as you can in the first three years. Talk and sing and do things with them. Teach them hygiene, one bath a day, brushing teeth at night before bed. Have set times for their breakfast, lunch, and dinner. Only one treat between meals. They learn fast and remember much.

When you have to work, try to be with them as much as possible. Believe me it will pay off in the end. Don't boss them around, but be aware of what's going on. Encourage them in everything they want to learn and do, but know what it is, so you can correct them and/or talk to them. They're not alone, they can trust you at all times. Teach them good habits and teach them to play well with other children. Show them at all times that you love them unconditionally.

COMPETITIONS

Oh yes, I come from a competitive family! My father was a harbor pilot, and my first competition was a bridge tournament for all the officers and their wives. I was pretty good too. So was my mother. My father played bridge, but he was not such a good player.

Everybody appreciated and liked my father a lot. So, he let my mother play with me while he played with another officer. I had just turned twelve, was the only "child." I was allowed to play because I was Piet Zeeman's daughter. There were three other ladies who played also. We had eighteen tables.

Mother and I were N and S. We played duplicate bridge, Culbertson system. We did well and were so excited. Sure enough, we came in as first and got the trophy and prize. We were so proud and happy, but some of the others weren't all that happy. After that it was only for adults.

The second time I won I was on the ship *Willem Ruis* from Indonesia to the Netherlands in 1949. Because my dad was an officer, we were in first class. Of course, we kids were mostly in second class.

We had deck tennis and table tennis on the deck of the ship. Sure enough, I won again in the singles and later in the doubles with my friend Tito.

On the same ship they had "horse races." One of my dad's friends wanted me to play for them. They threw one die and I had to move the horse. They gambled on it. Well, what do you know! I came in first. They won the money, but I was taken ashore in the next harbor for a trip AND a gift. Oh yes, I was very competitive and lucky when I was young.

In Holland we played table tennis. I played with my co-workers, people from church, and other students at evening school. I usually won, but the games at work were the most fun because we played against other companies, in other cities. It was so much fun. Everyone was so proud of me. I never was good in school, had to study so hard to make it, just by an inch. And they often teased me badly. But I always won the competitions!

One Easter at church, my boyfriend and I played table tennis. We each played a singles game, and together a doubles game. We won it all and went home with five dozen eggs. Everybody was so happy. We had enough eggs to eat, color, and hide. The whole family was happy.

In Canada we played tennis in the summer and played bridge and went bowling in the winter. I played bridge with my mother again and we often won. That was a good time. Some of my sisters and my brother Jan played too, but I was the stronger player. I guess I always had to prove to myself that I was as good as they were.

Only Letty, my sister, could play tennis like the best. She always did her utmost because she had to show what she could do it in spite of having had polio. Her left leg was shorter than her right. She's a very strong person, mentally and physically. She's eighty years old now, can still stand on her head! We all like to dance and try to outdo each other all the time. But always in fun, honestly, and proudly. We are always happy for the winner.

When my dad was young, he played soccer in Holland and mother played tennis. They taught us to play, be happy and do our best. We never had to look far for a partner. One of the advantages of having a big family.

Even in school I competed! Yes, I couldn't follow the HBS (high school) in Holland. That's true because of my late start after the war. Yet, I finished four years of business college at night in Holland while working full time. In Canada I did grade twelve over in English and made it. I also took French, public speaking, and some other courses for fun.

My biggest challenge was here in the United States. I'm really only a trained office worker. Because I had to make more money to raise my children, I took several extra jobs, such as selling Tupperware, Amway, Mary Kay, and Sovereign House Crystal that later became Princess House Crystal. I was so good at selling Princess House Crystal that I bought my house from the money I made. Then disaster came. I had an ugly gallbladder operation and I had to start all over again.

This time I took up Respiratory Therapy, did the very difficult two-year course in thirteen months. Even my teacher said, "Quit, Maria, it's too difficult for you at this age and with all the responsibilities you have." But I completed it!

Later on, when this profession needed to be officially recognized as a medical profession, I needed a certificate. I had to take the final exam over again. Yes, I failed the first time, but I made it the second time. I was so proud of myself. I did this work until my sixtieth birthday when I retired.

Now I can slow down, do things I like. Think about things I've put aside. I feel that I've done my utmost with my children and family. It's time for me now. I want to play bridge again, write my stories and have more friends, people to talk to and do fun things with. I'm trying to do just that now. I don't have to be the best anymore! I'm just happy to be able to still do things well.

RAIN, RAIN, OH RAIN!

What many mixed feelings I have about rain. When I was a kid in Indonesia, it would sometimes rain hard like cats and dogs. Sometimes it would only rain across the street. It was not cold and we would race there and enjoy it. But it was all over in about half an hour. So, we waited until the "water from the sky" would come again. What joy we had.

When I was in Holland, France, or Belgium, it seemed to rain all day! Not hard, but softly, sometimes only big drops. And it was cold. Brrr. I didn't like that at all. Sometimes it would rain hard, and the wind would blow so hard that we lost our umbrellas and hats, sometimes our balance! Then there was lightning and thunder! Very exciting, but also scary. My grandfather, years ago, lost his eye during such a storm. My sister-in-law's father lost his life working in the tulip fields. On top of that I was not allowed to look at the sky and I had to come in right away. It wasn't much fun.

I also was in Seattle. It's a fascinating city and a very beautiful state. It also seemed to rain all the time, but softly.

Vancouver, Canada, was the same. Such beautiful flowers and green everywhere, but where is the sun? My sister lived there for many years and I went often to enjoy all the beauty for a little while. But I had to go back to California! I love the sun at all times. It makes me feel happy and energetic. Rain depresses me, I don't want to do anything.

I should be happy with the rain here in California. We desperately need it. It's good for us. But soon we have the SUN again.

Let's be happy with what we have!!

HALLOWEEN STORY

I think Halloween is one of the nicest celebrations. Where I come from, it's not known. When I first came to the US with my girls, three and six years old, they were so excited from all the stories they heard, and the books that I read to them. Halloween is great!

I made the girls' costumes. Bea was a Spanish dancer with a very wide skirt with many colors. She loved it and wore it long after Halloween. For Loretta I made a real pretty cowboy outfit. She loved it too.

Loretta and Beatrix with costumes I made

They went to our neighbors and friends, coming home with a bag full of goodies, many scary stories, and very excited. It became their favorite holiday. We celebrated it every year. I made many outfits until they left my house.

Then we had fun with their children. But as time progressed it wasn't so much fun and popular anymore until we went to celebrate it in the park. That's still fun but not the same. They play games to win candies, have a costume contest, cakewalk, and more. At that time, I was working and I made many clown outfits to sell. That was fun and profitable.

Today, almost everybody in the family is too big for trick-or-treating. They go to dance parties and such. I stay home most of the time, give out some candies, and just reminisce quietly. That is nice too.

MINDLESS

One day I had to have my blood drawn. I couldn't eat or drink anything for twelve hours. So, I went early to that lab on Painter in the city of Whittier. The room was full of people. Many weren't even sitting. I just walked in and straight out again. What a disappointment. I can't wait that long. So, I went home.

I had an appointment for twelve thirty, but my nephew was coming at lunchtime, so I thought I would just go early to have my lab work done. It didn't work out.

When I was home, I did my chores, mainly outside with my plants and animals. I didn't eat or drink anything. When my nephew came, I served him but I had to stay without food or drink. After he left, I took the car, went to the lab for my appointment. I was a little late, so I had to wait anyway.

I was driving around and around, didn't know where I was, didn't know where I was going. Everything looked strange. Cars and cars and people everywhere. I worked myself up into a total panic. I thought I had lost my mind. I was going into a total panic attack. When I was young, I often had dreams that I was lost. There were always lots of people. I was always going, sometimes down stairs or sometimes just dirt roads. The people looked at me strangely and were scary. Down, down, I went, past many dark wooden doors that were closed. So scary looking, so dark, so scary!

Why did I think of that now? Here are cars and people everywhere.

Where am I going, I wondered. I'm just going home, but where do I live? Oh God help me. All strangers and they just look at me. No friendly looks, so scary! I stop in front of a liquor store, just sitting in my car. What's happening, God, what is the reason for this? Please help me find my way. Please help me find a friendly person.

Tears are dripping down my cheeks. I have to get out of this car, what can I do? Some people look at me. No friends. Is this when you lose your mind? Oh dear, this man comes, is in a hurry, but he stops and stares at me, then he comes close and reaches out to me. His eyes change to friendly eyes. He asks if he could help me, I don't know. I just stare at him. He's going. Oh no, maybe he's a good guy.

Lord, help me what to do. Then I said, "I'm lost." He turned and said, "Where were you going?" I had the lab slip in my hands, but there wasn't an address on. I told him, "I'm lost, I went there a hundred thousand times. I don't know where I am. I'm losing my mind."

He came close and said, "I get lost too sometimes, don't worry, let me look at your slip of paper."

"There's no address on it. It's somewhere in Whittier," I said.

He went to another stranger and asked if they knew where that lab was. He didn't know either. Then he asked someone in the car, a lady, and she knew it! My stranger told me how to get there.

I did finally arrive there—two hours and fifteen minutes after I left my house!

It's normally a fifteen-minute drive. When I came to the room, there wasn't a single person there except the workers. They noticed something was wrong and helped me right away. I told them, "I was lost." Then one of the technicians came and talked to me.

"What!" he said, "you didn't eat or drink anything since last night at nine o'clock? That's why you were lost, your blood sugar is so low. As soon as we have your specimens, you need to eat and drink something."

The moral of this story is never stop eating and/or drinking for more than twelve hours or you might get "mindless."

A MINI VACATION TO LOS ANGELES

My daughter Loretta and her girlfriend Michelle invited me to spend a day and a night in Los Angeles. Well, I thought that would be nice, even though I've been there many times. It didn't sound so exiting but I said, "I'll be happy to join you."

They picked me up with a Starbucks coffee (my favorite) and snacks for in the car. Lately it's very congested on the I-5 Freeway and the 101 no matter what time you go. The first stop was at the Western Bonaventure Hotel. A beautiful, very tall building. On the main floor is a restaurant, very interesting, decorated, and the next floor has several specialty stores, an LA Fitness, and more.

But we wanted to go on the glass elevators, which showed us a fantastic view of Los Angeles. On top of the building there is a gorgeous restaurant that turns all around so that one can see comfortably all over LA. Next, we went to a museum in Chinatown.

They had great paintings and many on velvet. They were very interesting too. I never actually saw those on velvet before. It's like the person or object is coming out of the painting. One had a flower in her hand, it looked like she was giving it to me. There was one of an old man smoking a cigarette, and it looked like the smoke was coming right out of the picture.

There were lots of very good paintings of Elvis Presley, David Bowie, Santana, Doris Day, several of Michael Jackson, one of Obama as a young man, and many, many more. All fabulous. There were also, some funny ones and a whole room of black light posters that glowed. Really spectacular to see.

Then we went to a nice restaurant in Koreatown for lunch. Had lobster and Korean noodles that were out of this world. The brussels sprouts were also delicious. We walked through the LA County Central Public Library. An interesting building, very big with many different rooms with all kinds of books. There were special sections for women or men, children and teenagers. All with special Help desks with a person. It was very impressive. But we didn't stay too long because we realized that we could spend the rest of the day there. There was more to see and do.

We had to see the OUE Skyscape at the US Bank Tower downtown and we rode the elevator to the seventieth floor! It has a premium event space (estimated 3,600 sq. ft.). It's the tallest building West of the Mississippi River, eleventh tallest in North America and sixty-fifth tallest in the world. We went down to the sixty-ninth floor. There are two open-air observation terraces to look all over the city. We could even see the Hollywood sign. Cars looked like toys and people were tiny. It was fantastic. I never realized what a great city LA is.

This building also has a sky-slide thrill attraction outside, and enclosed with clear plastic. We watched as people slid down from the seventieth floor to where we were standing. Of course, Loretta had to do it. I went back upstairs with her. She made me go first. Oh boy, it looked so scary, but I had to do it. It was over in no time!! I did it, but not anymore!! Michelle didn't want to do it, but I said, "Girl, I did it and you have to do it too." She did. It was exciting and fun.

After that we were tired. Thank goodness they had reserved a room at a bed-and-breakfast in Hollywood Hills, which wasn't far. There were two beds and a bathroom. So, we could rest, take a bath and change into evening clothes. It was nice and comfortable.

The next event was dinner—oysters and lobster (I had crab) at Rockwell Table and Stage. We saw a fun show, a musical parody of "Mean Girls." The singing was good. I had some wine too. Then we went back to our rooms in Hollywood Hills. The next morning, they had a fabulous breakfast, for us, better than in most hotels or motels and we drove home. An absolutely unforgettable day in LA.

MY BEDROOM

My bedroom is large. I had it built on to the back of the house. My big window looks out at the yard. Standing in front of my window I can see my many flowers and vegetable plants on the left, several trees, bird feeders, and bird houses. On the right I have my Jacuzzi, covered and cozy. You will find me there several times a week, enjoying it and doing exercises, or laying around on my lounge chair reading a book.

My double bed is in the left corner against the wall. There is a beautiful rug with the image of a lion above it. Near the bottom of the bed is a night stand with the television, next to that my vanity set. A door to the bathroom. Next to the door is my china cabinet with nice crystal, dinnerware, many family pictures, and souvenirs of my travels. I have many pictures on the wall. Next to that is a bookcase, also filled with souvenirs, pictures, and memorabilia.

Then we have the door to the hallway. To the left is my office with my computer, a copier, and two small tables. Above my desk are book shelves on the wall. Next to my computer is a door to get out. To the right is another bookcase. Back to the hallway to the right is the living room. I love my roomy bedroom.

MY PRECIOUS ONE

I have had you for more than seven years. You have pleased me always. From the beginning you gave flowers, sometimes two or three, and once, seven. They're so beautiful. But this year you outdid yourself! Thirty-two flowers, all big and glorious, white with a yellow heart--on my birthday! I'm so thankful for all the beauty you give.

Some people say that you don't have feelings and don't know what goes on. Well, I'm sure that you, my precious cactus plant, know me. I'm the one who talks to you, gives you bigger pots, new soil. waters you with just the right amount. I look to you every morning full of hope and praise for your special flowers to make the world beautiful and my day happy.

EXTENDED "FAMILY"

LIKE MOTHER, LIKE DAUGHTER

I'm looking at this picture of my mother and my sister with Mother's dog Dolly and her cat Beauty. She got the cat first when she worked at Montreal General Hospital. Beauty was a very small kitten, found between the walls of the hospital. Others didn't know what to do with that little grayish "thing," but my mother knew, she took it home.

When I saw the little cat, I liked it a lot. But I didn't think it was good to have a cat in the house with a newborn baby. I was living then with my mother, my daughter Loretta, my new baby Beatrix, and my sister Trixie and her son Danny.

My mother was so taken with the kitten that she said, "Don't worry, I keep her in my room." So, I had to agree with it. Beauty turned out to be the best cat anyone could ever have. She was not only attached to mother, but also, to my displeasure at first, to my newborn daughter Beatrix. Beauty found her spot under Beatrix's crib and slept there from her very first night. She came out when my mother was there, but as soon as Beatrix was put in her crib, the cat was back under it. Later Bea could do whatever she wanted with her and had never a scratch.

But Beauty was my mother's cat and she knew it. When we left Canada, my mother kept the cat and later, when she moved in with my sister Trixie, the cat came too. Beauty lived until she was twenty-three years old. We all loved her. She lived with Mother until she died a peaceful death next to my mother's bed.

Mother also got a dog, Dolly. It was a Chihuahua mix. White and very small, four pounds. My mother took her everywhere. She took her to the restaurants, stores, movies, on the plane to Holland, the US, and more. She was my mother's little sweetheart.

My dad passed away when he was only sixty-two years old, my mother lived until she was ninety-five. She got her physical love not only from her children, but daily from her Beauty and Dolly. We, her eight children, joked and teased her, in a loving way, about her Dolly a lot.

When I moved to California with my two girls, we soon had

a cat again. Beatrix loves cats. Guillermo, my son, loves dogs, so we had them too. They got along fine. Soon our cat had five kittens!

Beatrix wanted to keep them all! She could play with the kittens and the mother cat did nothing to her. When my son or Loretta touched them, she got mad and scratched them, which made them real sad.

We were able to give three kittens to another home. Soon we moved to Norwalk, a city not far away. We now had three cats, a dog, and a bird. The bird was in a cage and the cats got along fine with Prince, Guillermo's dog. The mother cat was always with Beatrix. When Bea went to school, a block and a half away, the silly cat walked with her and then returned home. We all loved our animals.

Beatrix always had cats, but later, on when she was on her own, she got a dog too. Always big dogs. When her last cat and dog died of old age, Beatrix had nothing for a while. Now she has a smaller dog, Jenny. Jenny's face looks like a Chihuahua, her body like a wiener dog. Beatrix loves her and wants no more animals.

Now, at age eighty-two, I have my Honey, a miniature Yorkshire terrier. She will be fourteen years old in October this year. She's blind, deaf, hasn't got a tooth in her month, and can hardly walk. Many tell me, "Why not put her down?" But she never whines or seems unhappy, only now very needy. Two years ago, she was still fine, and I took her everywhere on most of my outings and trips.

She's only two pounds now, I still take her with me often, but not everywhere. She's content to be home, sitting next to my thigh while I read or watch television. I take her for a walk in her stroller and shop with her in my sling. My kids joke and tease me now, too. I hope also in a loving way!

Written 2017

HOW I MET MY HONEY

About thirteen years ago, my daughter Loretta got a teacup Yorkshire terrier. He was so small and he looked like a drowned little rat when he was born. He only weighed one and a half pounds. We never had such a small dog. We really liked him, and we called him Lucas. He grew until he was three and a half pounds. He was the joy in our house.

But Loretta moved to Minnesota and took Lucas with her. I went there several times to visit. Lucas was trying to get used to the extreme cold. Loretta took him to work and he sat under her desk in a small dog bed with a warmer. At home, Loretta did the same for him.

One day a botfly laid its eggs in his eye!!! He got deathly ill, but by an absolute shamanic miracle, he got better. This is a story for another time.

One day, when Loretta was at a park in Minnesota, a lady asked if she wanted another Yorkie because she had one she did not want.

Loretta said, "Let me come and see her first." She did, and what a sorry sight it was!

She saw a little two-pound dog with many bald spots and matted, dirty hair, and very sickly. The lady said, "This is my daughter's dog, but she left to a university and left the dog with me and I can't take care of her." Indeed, she didn't. She had a small room for the dog with a big bowl of food and water and newspapers all over the floor. She left her there for days. The dog never came out.

It was awful. Loretta took her straight to a vet and then to a groomer. After that she didn't look so bad, but she was obviously sick. The vet said, "She's very neglected. If you don't keep her and take special care of her, she won't live more than a few months." Loretta took her to my home, which was difficult on the plane.

When I looked at her, I was at first shocked, but then I looked into her beautiful eyes and fell totally in love with her. I realized that she'd be mine forever to keep. I'd make her better, prettier, and show her that she's worthy of love and care. Her big brown eyes looked at me with such trust and adoration.

How could I ever not accept her the way she is now, neglected, skinny, with many bald spots on her body. Oh, little love, I will make you beautiful and full of happy spirit. You will run and know that I adore you.

I promised to take good care of her. We named her "Honey." I gave her fish oil for more than a month every day. She smelled like fish. Some of my grandkids were calling her "Oma's fish dog." Her hair came back beige and black, she gained weight, was livelier, and seemed happy.

She has the looks now, pretty and proud. She bosses me around in such a cute way that I love her more for it. Her other companions love her too and actually she rules our house now. My little three and a half--pound Yorkie gives a little "woof" or touches our arm or hand with her little paw, and we all are in action.

"What is it, Honey, you want to go out and pee? You want a little snack? You want some loving? Come, little one, and you shall have it."

She now eats well, just about everything, always wanting a small piece of whatever we eat. She eats with gusto. I think that she then remembers her "old" life.

Loretta's dog Lucas is very picky with his food, often needs special food. I have Honey now about seven years, she's a little picky too now. She doesn't like soft food, but with no teeth it's difficult for her. So, I always make her food in very small pieces and give her freeze-dried food.

Honey became inseparable from me. She sleeps in my bed. I made a small ladder so she can go up or down. I take her almost everywhere, to the park, visiting friends, going on trips, even to Canada when one of my nieces got married. She's so good, sweet and lovable. She often sits in her bag or stroller when I go out.

I'm never short of attention with her. People, young and old, often children, stop, want to see her close by, tell me how pretty she is, ask questions, and talk to me.

I always had big dogs. I loved them too, but now that I'm older, I really love and enjoy our small dogs. Lucas is four and a half pounds; Honey is three and a half pounds. My Honey will be fourteen years old in October.

(l-r) Lucas, Hero, and Honey

LUCAS – OUR LITTLE "HOUDINI"

One day I was dog-sitting with Lucas while Loretta was at a conference in Sacramento. I took him with me to Beatrix's dance studio in Garden Grove and he escaped out the front door.

I stayed outside waiting for news. I was in charge of him and I didn't know what happened. Three teenagers were outside the studio. They said they saw a little dog running away. They followed him on their bikes and wanted to bring him back to the area where they found him. Then a car stopped and the driver said, "Hey, guys, that's my dog." So, they gave the woman the dog.

I jumped in the car after I heard that and tried to find the car that the boys described. An hour later I came back and told all the people in the studio that I wouldn't leave and would wait until I had him back. The whole class in my daughter's dance studio went out to help look for him. We put up flyers and offered $300 for his return. We called the police because Lucas had been stolen. I stayed late into the evening, then went home, defeated.

In the mean time I decided to call my daughter, Loretta. I waited until about nine o'clock and gathered my courage to call her. She was obviously upset. She wanted to make plans to come home, but she had to make a presentation the next morning.

The next day I got a call from Loretta. She said, "I got a call that Lucas is in a shelter in Costa Mesa. What's happening?" She said that the police had been looking for our little four-pound Yorkie and by a miracle, they saw him walking on the sidewalk in Costa Mesa, fifty miles away from home. He was shivering and scared. They had no problem taking him to the shelter.

The shelter people checked his chip (thank God we put a chip in our pets) and called Loretta's cell phone. They said, "Please pick your dog up, ASAP."

I raced to the shelter and went right in where the little dogs were. But NO LUCAS. When I went to the office they said, "He's right there," but I said, "No, he isn't."

Then another person said, "Oh, you're looking for that little Houdini. He managed to escape from two closed places for small dogs so we put him with the big dogs. The gates are much sturdier there and after a while he just gave up. None of the big dogs even paid any attention to him, luckily."

When he saw me, he whined. I never heard him whine like that. Oh, my heart broke in two from despair for him. And then, I couldn't pick him up yet because they insisted that they needed proof of a rabies shot. I did not have his papers with me. At six thirty in the morning the vet's office wasn't open yet. So, I told them, "Just give it to him!" Then I picked him up and all my waiting and agonies were over. He licked my lips and I kissed my little boy and took him home to Loretta.

Our little "Houdini"

I SWEAR LUCAS HAS NINE LIVES

I swear that my daughter's doggie has nine lives. I will tell you about one of them! Lucas is a four-pound adorable Yorkshire terrier teacup dog. He's smart, playful, and we take him everywhere with us. He sits in "his" bag very quietly when we are in a restaurant or seeing a movie, listens well when we are in the park or at friends.

One evening we came home rather late and sent Lucas out in the yard to do his business. When he came in the house, he looked stricken at Loretta and fell down. She looked at him and saw that a bee had stung him in the mouth. The bee was still there. She removed it. But Lucas looked like he was not breathing and almost comatose.

She called the animal hospital that was open twenty-four hours and rushed him in. The doc gave him Benadryl, put an I.V. in and placed him in an incubator. He told us there wasn't much hope for him to survive. If he does, he might have extensive brain damage.

We sat with him a few hours when I told Loretta to go home, come back in the morning. When she came back, there was no improvement. She cried and her son came over to support her, and then two girlfriends. All five big people stood around this little three and a half-pound dog in the smallest incubator I ever saw.

The doctor said that we could put our hand through the hole of the incubator and touch our Lucas to say good bye. We barely all fit in that room but we all had a turn. Then the others left and I decided to stay until the end.

Loretta was coming back later for me. It was in the middle of the morning and another doctor came in and said, "If only he would take a crumb or some water from your finger. That's the only thing you can do for him." And I put a drop on my finger and what do you know! I saw his nose smelling it! He took a tiny little lick. And lo and behold! He actually survived! He is a little lopsided and unbalanced now, but so are we. HAHAHA It seemed like another miracle had happened!

MY HONEY WAS LOST!

Yes!! I got my little three and a half-pound Yorkshire terrier dog back! We were at an event in my daughter's dance studio for one hour when I had to go to the restroom. I take my little Honey just about everywhere—to the movies, store, restaurant, bus, airplane etc. Honey is not just a dog, she's my support dog. She's my emotional support dog.

I asked Bea, "Watch her, I won't be long," and I ran to the restroom. When I came out, my other daughter Loretta said, "Where is Honey? She ran right after you but then took a detour and ran out the door of the studio. I don't see her anywhere. She had at the most a forty-second had start. She should be right here."

We looked and looked. Inside the studio they heard that Honey was missing. Many people came outside the studio to help us to look for Honey. We put hand-written notices out, but no Honey. I was devastated. I called the police. Two police cars came and they would look also and call if something came up. They were very sorry and kind, but couldn't do much about a lost dog.

After more than three hours, we all gathered in front of the studio It was already eleven o'clock at night. Everybody was ready to depart. I was terribly upset and said, "No, I will stay here and wait!"

And, what do you know! A car passed by and the driver asked, "Are you looking for a little dog?" They held Honey out of the window. Everybody cheered.

I was so relieved and happy to have her back. Honey was fine and the couple in the car said that they had picked her up from the street in front of the studio, went to eat something and passed by where they had picked her up earlier to see if somebody lost a dog. I gave them what I had in my wallet and thanked them profusely. I consider myself a very lucky person and I will never leave my Honey again, not even for one minute.

MY HONEY

One day, my beloved daughter brought me this little Yorkie. She didn't look very healthy, but she looked me in the eyes and I fell in love with her. Loretta got her from an older lady who never really took care of her.

We took her to a vet who advised us not to take her because she wouldn't live more than a few months. But I did take her in. She became my sweetheart. She had not felt or seen grass before, she loved it. She got small plates with a little food that she liked. I could see how happy she was and how much healthier she became. I took her everywhere with me, to the park, movie, restaurant, visiting family and places. She was so good. I had a small stroller for her and a sling if she wanted to be carried. She was my support dog. In many ways. I needed her as much as she needed me.

I had her for ten and a half years. In time she lost all her teeth, later her eye sight. Then she could no longer hear. But she kept going for over eight years. She fell on our vacation in Canada and she got worse. She could hardly walk anymore.

One night she sat next to me on the coach. I held her and cried, but by morning she got a little better. After a few weeks she was with me in my bed with a blanket over her and me too. She really tried hard to be healthy and good for me. She knew I needed her as much as she needed me.

But this time she felt so cold. I held her close, praying and getting sad. In the morning I called my daughters and they both came. We all three were with her. She didn't leave my sight on the couch. She never licks much, but I felt her little tongue on my upper leg. Oh God let her stay with me a little longer! By six o'clock the girls went home and Honey was still alive.

Two hours later she felt really cold again and she almost stopped breathing. I was immensely sad, called the girls, and they came back. But Honey actually died in my arms.

I was grief-stricken! I never felt that bad!

I lost my father, mother, three sisters and two brothers. I was with them until the end and I was very sad, but I knew where they were going. Some say that I would see them again.

But my Honey, she was as much my angel as I was for her. You might think, "She's only a dog!" Yet, that dog was my family and I was so depressed. I had a very hard time with it. I cried for days every time I would think, see, or hear about her.

We buried her and prayed for her. I sat at her grave for almost four hours and I'm still heart broken. That's why I write this, so my Honey knows how much she meant to me and how much I loved this little sweet dog.

THE END – BUT NOT YET

This is the end of my book, but not of me. I am now eighty-four, and I have lived an amazingly full life. Only Letty and I are still here. I look back on these stories, and I think I will put them in a book for you, my loved ones, to enjoy. I hope you will get to know me a little better, and perhaps learn some things you never knew. Remember, a life well lived has scars and messy memories. That is what makes it all so interesting.

Written 2019

EDITOR'S NOTE

The devastation of Europe and northern Asia brought about by World War II was widely known in the United States. US military forces participated in the fighting on many fronts and in the liberation of prisoners held in Nazi concentration camps.

European rebuilding was in the news for many years afterwards. Television and print ads from humanitarian organizations encouraged Americans to donate Care packages for refugees and displaced persons.

Americans also fought in southern Asia, including Burma, Malaysia, and Indonesia, where the war was equally devastating. But in contrast, comparatively few Americans were aware of what civilians experienced in that part of the globe. While Maria's personal story is unique, her experience symbolizes the brutality suffered by millions of innocent people throughout the region.

It is not surprising that when Maria sought counseling, she encountered several professionals who told her that they had never heard about the events in Indonesia or the prison camps.

Modern technology and the internet are correcting this paucity of information about the Asian theater of World War II. People are writing blogs, uploading videos and pictures, publishing memoirs, and connecting with other survivors. They are finding validation as they share their stories with the world.

For those who would like to know more about this period of Indonesian history, a Google search for "Tjideng," the main camp, will bring up dozens of images and sites with information—some scholarly, many personal.

A Google search for Captain Kenichi Sonei, the brutal and notorious leader of Tjideng camp described by Maria, quickly reveals that he was executed for war crimes on December 7, 1946.

A YouTube search for "Tjideng" is also fruitful, offering almost a dozen videos.

Also by Los Nietos Press

Star Chasing, Thomas R. Thomas (2019)

Dancing in the Santa Ana Winds: Poems y Cuentos New and Selected, liz gonzález (2018)

California Trees, Kit Courter (2018)

Wingless, Linda Singer (2017)

Sharing Stories: Global Voices Coming Together, Various Authors (2016)

The Beatle Bump, Clifton Snider (2016)

Yearlings, Frank Kearns (2015)

So Cali, Trista Dominqu (2015)

Persons of Interest, Lorine Parks (2015)

ABOUT LOS NIETOS PRESS

Los Nietos Press is dedicated to the countless generations of people whose lives and labor created the world community that today spreads over the coastal floodplain known simply as Los Angeles.

We take our name from the Los Nietos Spanish land grant that was south and east of the downtown area. Our purpose is to serve local writers so they may share their words with many, in the form of tangible books that can be held and read and passed on. This written art form is one way we realize our common bonds and help each other discover what is meaningful in life.

LOS NIETOS PRESS
www.LosNietosPress.com
LosNietosPress@Gmail.com

Made in the USA
San Bernardino, CA
07 January 2020